A SUSSEX CHRISTMAS

Sussex shepherd, 1925. (Garland Collection)

A SUSSEX CHRISTMAS

FRAN & GEOFF DOEL

The History Press

*To the affectionate memory of Geoff's grandparents,
George and Florrie Mitchell, licensees of the Queensbury Arms
(The Hole in the Wall), Brighton, around 1924-56,
who introduced him to the delights of Sussex ale.*

First published 2025

The History Press
97 St George's Place, Cheltenham,
Gloucestershire, GL50 3QB
www.thehistorypress.co.uk

British Library Cataloguing in Publication Data.
A catalogue record for this book is available from the British Library.

ISBN 978 1 83705 011 6

Typesetting and origination by The History Press.
Printed and bound in Great Britain by TJ Books, Padstow, Cornwall.

MIX
Paper | Supporting responsible forestry
FSC® C013056

The History Press proudly supports
Trees for Life
www.treesforlife.org.uk

EU Authorised Representative: Easy Access System Europe
Mustamäe tee 50, 10621 Tallinn, Estonia
gpst.request@easproject.com

CONTENTS

THE AUTHORS

Fran and Geoff Doel are retired university adult education lecturers in literature, medieval and cultural studies. Geoff is a Sussex man with a literary PhD and Fran has an MA in Medieval Studies. They have published 20 books, many of them for The History Press, and Geoff has appeared on *Time Team*.

ACKNOWLEDGEMENTS

We are very grateful for help and inspiration from a large number of Sussex dwellers past and present, in particular to the following individuals: Colin Andrews for use of his published material on Michael Blann; Andrew Barlow, Keeper of the Royal Pavilion; John Bleacher for West Gallery recordings; Janie Bishop for memories of the ice cream cake; Sandra Collins, Assistant Ship Keeper at Hastings Fishermen's Museum; Rebecca Graham, House Steward, Nymans Garden; June Longly for her memories of the Brighton bombing; Sylvia Peters; Alison McCann, Assistant County Archivist, West Sussex Record Office; Margaret Stankiewicz, Acting Archivist for Lancing College; Peter Thorogood, owner of St Mary's, Bramber, for permission to use his poem; and Kathy Woollett, Assistant in Charge, Reference Library, Hastings Library.

Our thanks are also due to the very helpful librarians and staff at the following: Brighton Jubilee Library, Chichester Library, Lewes Library, Hastings Library, Tonbridge Library, the East Sussex Record Office, Lewes, and the West Sussex Record Office (in particular Mrs Alison McCann, the Assistant County Archivist), Chichester, the Sussex Archaeological Society and the Vaughan Williams Memorial Library of the English Folk Dance and Song Society.

We should also like to thank the West Sussex Record Office for allowing the inclusion of certain illustrations in their possession from the Garland Collection for which they hold the copyright.

With thanks also to the *Petworth Society Magazine* for permission to use the photograph 'Wassailing at Duncton in the late nineteenth century', also used in our book *Mumming, Hoodening and Howling: Midwinter Rituals in Sussex, Kent and Surrey.*

We should like to thank the Sussex Archaeological Society Library for permission to use material from the K.H. Macdermott manuscripts and the painting on the front cover, and the Vaughan Williams Memorial Library for access to, and use of, the Clive Carey notebooks and John Broadwood's *Old English Songs*.

A number of books, listed in the bibliography, have been particularly helpful in directing us to primary sources and illustrations and in background information, for which our thanks to the authors and publishers.

A Christmas display at Coppard's, No. 53 High Street, Lewes, 1878.

INTRODUCTION

Christmas celebrations in Sussex are rooted in a blend of Germanic paganism and enthusiastic early Christianity. Wassailing was noted in the north of the county in the nineteenth century and the Yule log and apple wassailing survived on the Weald and at the village of Duncton respectively until the early twentieth century. The singing of Christmas carols both succeeded and incorporated the wassail tradition. An interesting example of the blend is *The Sussex Wassail* song, the tune of which was reused for the famous carol *God Rest Ye Merry Gentlemen*. The Christmas evergreens and mistletoe also originally relate to pagan midwinter, solstitial and New Year celebrations which were taken over by emerging Christianity. Feasting is another element of the ancient Yule festivities which has survived into medieval and modern Christian Christmas celebrations. Ashby's, the Haywards Heath grocer, supplied ice cream cake on Christmas Day just after the Second World War.

No county has a richer tradition of mummers' plays than Sussex and their survival and revival have also been stronger than elsewhere, with the exception of Kent. It can be confidently asserted that a play was performed somewhere in Sussex in virtually every year of the twentieth century except for wartime. The early death and resurrection formula of these plays could also stem from Germanic paganism, but the subject matter of the texts is essentially medieval, that of crusading Christians against Muslim Turks. The actual texts are later still, probably evolving orally in village productions and we have included the earliest Sussex references to mummers, some of which were first published in our book

Mumming, Howling and Hoodening: Midwinter Rituals in Sussex, Kent and Surrey.

Rudyard Kipling's famous poem *Eddi's Service* excellently captures the spirit of the earliest Anglo-Saxon phase of Sussex Christianity, connected with the conversion of parts of Sussex by St Wilfrid. But there was an earlier Celtic missionary, Dicul at Bosham, who was perhaps the first to celebrate the midwinter Christmas in Sussex. The thirteenth-century local saint, Bishop Richard of Chichester, really caught the Sussex imagination with a series of dramatic miracles, such as the proliferation of fish by the old Ouse Bridge at Cliffe in Lewes, and we have included a miraculous Christmas cure at Richard's tomb in Chichester Cathedral, the most important Sussex pilgrimage site. The Normans built Chichester Cathedral and also a number of fine castles in Sussex, many of which have seasonal traditions and apparitions; the Bramber Castle Christmastide haunting by starving children is the most sombre of these tales. Another Christmas-tide supernatural occurrence relates to the murderers of Archbishop Thomas à Becket, who fled to Malling Manor just after the murder.

Consideration of the poor at Christmas is a Christian practice dramatised in *Good King Wenceslas*, composed by a Sussex minister, and exemplified in Christmas doles and charities and workhouse dinners. Other institutions, such as Lancing College, Brighton Hospital and Lewes Children's Homes, also had their own Christmas celebrations. Occupations such as shepherding and fishing had distinctive Christmas traditions. Boxing Day sports ranged from the Boxing Day Hunt to swimming in the sea at Brighton and regular Boxing Day fixtures for the Brighton and Hove Albion Football Club. Geoff, who is Sussex born, recalls playing cricket for Hove Wilbury on Christmas Day in the 1960s (once scoring – for him – a rare fifty on a very soggy wicket with bowlers bowling at half pace!). And skating is recorded at St Andrew's Garden, Bulverhythe, during the white Christmas of 1870.

Then there are the seasonal disasters, such as the famous Lewes avalanche and the destruction of Eastbourne Pier and Brighton Chain Pier. And the traditional Christmas weather sayings, such as a delightful one recorded from a shepherd's wife in the West Wittering Women's Institute: 'If the ice will bear a duck before Christmas, it won't bear a goose after'. Sussex is a county rich in collected and surviving folksong and there were a huge number of excellent Christmas songs for us to choose from, both from the well-documented West Gallery tradition and the secular collections.

Such is the wealth of Sussex traditional Christmas material that we have been able to avoid duplication (except in the essential case of Kipling) with Shaun Payne's excellent earlier Christmas anthology for the county (now out of print). It is because of Shaun's extensive use of the famous Copper family of Rottingdean, whom we much admire, that we have decided to use other singers and collectors in our anthology to reflect the widespread vitality and quality of Sussex folksong.

In the words of the Revd John Broadwood: 'May joy come to you and to our wassail'.

Fran and Geoff Doel
April 2005

The River Ouse, Lewes.

GOOD KING WENCESLAS

By John Mason Neale

This loved and frequently sung carol was written by a Victorian Sussex clergyman and hymn writer, John Mason Neale (1818-66), and was just one of a number of new hymns for the winter season he included in his 1853 publication Carols for Christmas-Tide. *After a spell as vicar of Crawley, Neale joined the staff as warden of the seventeenth-century almshouse, Sackville College, East Grinstead, in 1846, a post which carried a salary of £28 a year. His charges were thirty 'poor and aged' householders and he stayed in the post for twenty years until his death in 1866.*

The 'Victorian-style Christmas' was still a comparative novelty when this new carol was written. A new interest in the celebration of Christmas had been sparked off with Dickens' hugely popular story of the miser Scrooge and his conversion at Christmastime. Then came magazine reports of how Victoria celebrated Christmas at Windsor, with illustrations of the German Christmas tree illuminated with candles and hung with baubles This was a Germanic custom and had been introduced into the court by the young Queen's German consort, Albert; it would soon be adopted by Victoria's subjects. As the idea of Christmas as a family (as opposed to an important religious) (festival) grew in the popular imagination of Victoria's England, the first commercial Christmas card was designed and put on the market, but its production was expensive and only when the price fell did it become really popular. The invention of the Christmas cracker followed, and soon became part of the Christmas scene. Middle-class Victorian families also enjoyed gathering round a candlelit piano to sing the specially composed new seasonal hymns, such as Good King Wenceslas.

It is apparent that Neale was a compassionate man. The message inherent in his carol is that the coldest and bleakest time of year can occasion real suffering to the poor, therefore there is a special need for Christian charity at this period.

Neale set the action of Wenceslas' visit to the poor man appropriately on Boxing Day – St Stephen's Day – when the 'poor-boxes' in Victorian churches everywhere were opened up and money dispensed to the needy, and when traditionally the Victorian bourgeoisie, having already celebrated Christmas with the family, now dispensed tips to tradesmen and sent food to the parish poor. Though famous in his own country, Wenceslas was probably up to that point little known in England. An historical tenth-century ruler, he controlled part of what is now the Czech Republic; his birthplace was in a castle outside Prague. Famous for his charitable works, he was assassinated allegedly because of his attempts to introduce Christianity into the country.

Neale, who was a Latinist and lover of all things gothic, set his new hymn Good King Wenceslas *to the tune of a charming thirteenth-century spring carol, ostensibly a dancc tune, entitled* Tempus ad Floridum *(Spring has unwrapped her flowers). Here are the well-loved words; they were intentionally anachronistic:*

Good King Wenceslas looked out,
On the Feast of Stephen,
When the snow lay round about,
Deep and crisp and even.
Brightly shone the moon that night,

Though the frost was cruel,
When a poor man came in sight,
Gathering winter fuel.

'Hither, page, and stand by me,
If thou know'st it, telling,
Yonder peasant, who is he?
Where and what his dwelling?'
'Sire, he lives a good league hence,
Underneath the mountain,
Right against the forest fence,
By Saint Agnes' fountain.'

'Bring me food and bring me wine,
Bring me pine logs hither,
Thou and I will see him dine,
When we bear them thither.'
Page and monarch, forth they went,
Forth they went together,
Through the rude wind's wild lament,
And the bitter weather.

'Sire, the night is darker now,
And the wind blows stronger,
Fails my heart, I know not how;
I can go no longer.'
'Mark my footsteps, good my page,
Tread thou in them boldly,
Thou shalt find the winter's rage,
Freeze thy blood less coldly.'

In his master's steps he trod,
Where the snow lay dinted,
Heat was in the very sod,
Which the Saint had printed.
Therefore, Christian men, be sure,
Wealth or rank possessing,
Ye who now will bless the poor,
Shall yourselves find blessing.

Singing round the piano, c. 1870.
(Illustration from a Lewes magazine)

A Victorian illustration of
Good King Wenceslas.

CHRISTMAS DECORATIONS

At Christmastime the great houses, the churches and even the cottages of Sussex were decorated with all kinds of evergreen – holly, ivy, laurels, cypress, box, bay, rosemary and mistletoe – all available and often plentiful at that cold time of year and which in antiquity carried the symbolism of the renewal of the life force. The first literary mention of the Sussex 'Kissing Bough' or 'Kissing Bunch' – circles of suspended evergreen boughs formed into circles and decorated with candles and red apples, with mistletoe in the centre – appeared in the seventeenth century. The following reference concerns the making of Sussex garlands for a Christmas party in the early part of the twentieth century and comes from a tape recording made by Rebecca Graham, House Steward at Nymans, and taken from a National Trust interview in 2002 with Daphne Dengate, Secretary Companion to Mrs Maud Messel and her daughter, Anne, the Countess of Rosse. The Colonel living at Nymens at the time of the Christmas house party was Lieutenant Colonel Leonard Messel, who employed around twenty staff.

Daphne Dengate: 'Oh yes, there was one Christmas, they didn't do it again, when the Colonel asked all his sisters separately and their families to Christmas (at Nymans), and the gardeners were kept busy for weeks beforehand making garlands and they all hung right round the big hall.'

An early account of the decoration of churches in the nineteenth century comes from the pen of the Revd Edward Boys Ellman in his Recollections of a Sussex Parson:

When I was first ordained anything like church decoration was dreaded, the cross or even the candle-sticks on the altar was looked on as Popish. Flowers were considered the same. The only decoration ever indulged in was at Christmas. These decorations consisted of pieces of holly or other evergreens stuck on the tops of high pews, holes being bored in them to hold the branches...

I would add that Christmas was the only season before that I ever knew of any church being decorated. Gradually the other churches around were decorated also.*

About 1870, when church decorations were more thought of, the then Curate of Wilmington, the Rev. Samuel Ward, took great interest in the subject, and visited every church in the neighbourhood that he could, to see the Christmas decorations. He was told that the Arlington decorations were out of the common, so through rather deep snow he went to see them. He found great red flower-pots in each window, with a branch of evergreen stuck in each; nothing else. But he said the church walls were green with damp moss, and plants that had vegetated of their own accord were in the damp window-ledges. In the west window tall nettles were growing.

It was even a few years later that the Rector of West Dean (who then lived at Seaford), going over on a Christmas Day, found what the clerk styled 'Taxts' up. The 'Taxts' were three in number; what one was I forget. One was 'A Merry Christmas', over the altar, and the third consisted of three letters, 'M.B.P.'.

The Rector puzzled over in his mind during service as to what M.B.P. could mean and thought it must be something about the Virgin Mary. But the clerk explained that it was the initial letters of 'Mr. Bannister's Pew', and had been put up over that seat.

* In the early sixties (i.e. 1860s), amongst my earliest memories, are church decorations, seeing my father mark out texts and devices on white calico, which my mother, the village schoolmistress and my nurse worked over with leaves and flowers under his personal supervision. E.B. Ellman.

'The Home Decking to Welcome Christmas.' (Illustration from a Lewes magazine)

The rest of the decorations consisted of bent willow boughs across the aisle, from which dangled some oranges, which were afterwards to be given to children. The clerk was very proud of his decorations.

A rather less than enthusiastic report about decorating churches at Christmastime comes from the curate of Hamsay in the year 1871. From 'Parish Jottings', Lewes Churches Magazine, *Vol. VI:*

In our small parishes we are not all artists; and there is often amongst us a great gap between what we do and the effect produced. Some of us still live contentedly in the day of small things; and where a church has to be decorated year after year, probably by the same hands, a sort of stereotyped ornamentation is in vogue. Then we have some unhappy churches which all the decorations of Christendom would not enliven – churches with a hideous gallery jutting impertinently out into the body of the church – charity puts a text along its front, wraps it up as decently as it can; high pews, above which one sees a bit of ribbon belonging to somebody's bonnet, or a few hairs belonging to some male head. A pulpit so high up that any leaves on it would make it look like a holly tree – said pulpit having a sounding board over the preacher's head, as if the church were six times its size, and that the roof being leaky it required some protection for the preacher. Then, in some country churches, an insane notion of decoration is indulged by those who make little holes in the high pews, and insert pieces of holly into said holes, so that the worshippers on Christmas Day may suppose they are keeping Christmas Day in a young plantation! Then, how wonderfully fonts are decorated! Though many of them in small country parishes have quietly stepped out of observation into some remote corner. A great refuge to decorators is in texts! Great letters formed of holly and ivy leaves straddle across a black wall, and are better than nothing. Then when there are pillars to decorate we take the serpentine method, and wind a wreath round the stony corporation of the shaft – the top we encircle with another wreath. If we have windows we use the invariable moss for the base, and ivy round the sides. In some of our more pretentious churches all sorts of compromises are effected. Sham berries, sham leaves, letters of wool, rice, gold paper, imitation flowers and even imitation moss. There is no doubt about it that a young lady with taste will utilize a few sprigs of ivy and holly in the decoration of any part of a church; whereas another with all the wealth of a greenhouse would, without taste, merely make a flower show of her part of the work. Without design, and consequently without harmony – all decoration is so much maypole-work. Christmas decorators – 'Let all things be done decently and in order.'

There is more than one Sussex tradition regarding the disposal of greenery used as Christmas decoration. For some Twelfth Night ended with the taking down of all the evergreens and decorations, and to prevent bad luck it was stated that they must be burnt on this day. Others allowed the greenery to stay in situ until Candlemas.

'Grandpa under the mistletoe'. (Copyright Garland Collection, West Sussex Record Office)

CANDLEMAS DAY, 2 FEBRUARY

From the Lewes Churches Magazine, *Vol. II, 1868*

In the early Church, the ancient festival of Candlemas, which followed forty days after Christmas, marked the closure of the joyous Christmas and Epiphany season. During the Middle Ages it had evolved into a popular church service with a blessing of candles, when clergy and congregation, lighted candles in hand, moved in procession from the chuch to the graveyard outside.

Much later, numerous superstitions came to be associated with Candlemas. As this nineteenth-century Sussex account shows, it had become the day on which Christmas decorations of greenery were taken down and burned. Not to do so was thought to bring bad luck:

There were several curious customs connected with this season, one of which was the removal of the Christmas evergreens, though they might be replaced by the greener box until Easter. It was also the time appointed for the quenching of the Christmas log, and our forefathers must have been sensible of the lengthening days, for the use of candles which had been necessary at the evening services at church, during the dark winter, ceased from this time until Hallowe'en, 31 October. Hence the old saying:

On Candlemas Day
Throw candle and candlestick away.

A CHICHESTER CHRISTMAS MIRACLE

'Of the Cripple cured at St Richard's Tomb', from The Life of St Richard of Chichester *by Ralph Bocking*

As Bishop of Chichester, St Richard was renowned for the attention he paid to his pastoral duties, his concern for the poor and the holiness of his life. Chichester Cathedral was in desperate need of a local saint to encourage visits and donations from pilgrims and even before his death in 1253 it appears that his chaplain, Ralph Bocking, a Dominican friar and university-trained theologian, was collecting stories about miracles concerning the holy bishop. After his death the miracles continued and Ralph gives a selection of these in his The Life of St Richard of Chichester.

The canons of Chichester Cathedral assembled the documentation on the holiness of his life and on the miracles during and subsequent to his lifetime to apply to the pope for canonisation. The pope appointed three learned churchmen and scholars to investigate St Richard's merits and holiness. Forty witnesses testified to Richard's humility, nine witnesses testified that he did not care for fine clothes, expensive horses or rich trappings and nineteen testified that he acted with kindness and compassion towards the poor.

In the interim period before canonisation in 1262, Richard's grave in the north aisle of Chichester Cathedral was treated as a holy site and a chaplain appointed to tend it. In 1276, in a ceremony attended by King Edward I, St Richard was reburied in a silver-gilt shrine covered with jewels behind the high altar. A number of healing miracles occurred at his tomb and shrine. Ralph Bocking's The Life of St Richard of

Chichester *was completed in 1270, before the shrine was built, and therefore the tomb miracle outlined below is likely to have occurred at the tomb in the north aisle. The shrine was destroyed during the Reformation in 1538:*

There was a man named John Stokes living in the diocese of Chichester who, one day when he was at recreation with others, was suddenly stricken by paralysis, which affected the whole of his right side. He fell to the ground, immediately lost the use of the whole right half of his body and could not even get up without others to help him. The others took pity on the unfortunate man and carried him to a nearby house and there he remained paralysed

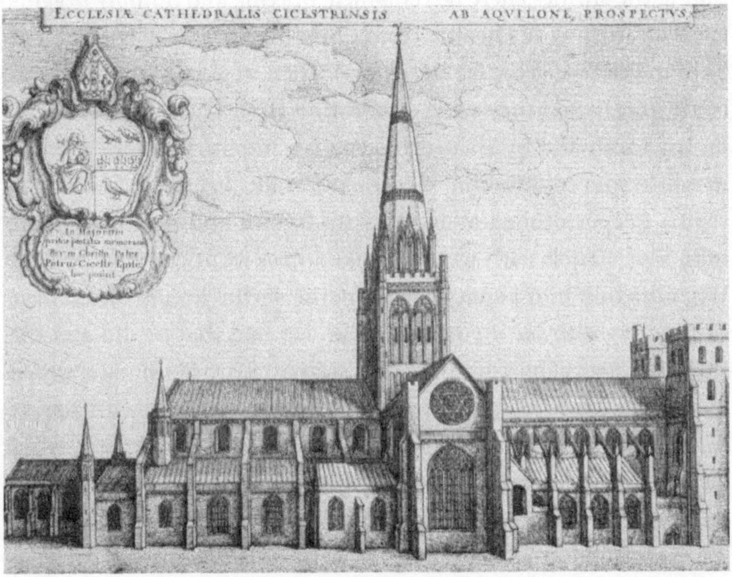

Chichester Cathedral from an engraving by Wenceslas Hollar.

for more than six years. His right hand and leg began to swell up and became pierced with many small holes which they called 'fistula'. His illness grew worse with each day that passed and the pus which trickled from his sores began to loosen his bones from his joints, to such an extent that several bones in his arm and leg seemed to be coming out with the putrid liquid. As he lay miserably afflicted in this way and with no help or medicine from doctors, reports of the blessed Richard's virtues began frequently to reach him. So, greatly spurred on by the hope that he could recover his health through the saint's glorious merits, with words, entreaties and in whatever other ways he could, he earnestly begged that somehow he should be taken to the saint's tomb. His host, who had afforded him hospitality in his house throughout his illness, took pity on his wretched state and, greatly moved by his cries, took him to the shrine. There he remained, praying and humbly begging for the return of his health, from Christmas Eve until the Feast of St John the Evangelist (27 December). Then, at about the third hour of the day, when they were celebrating High Mass, he fell asleep by the tomb and in his dreams saw an imposing figure dressed in white who said to him, 'Get up and walk.' When he awoke, the shrine-keeper immediately came up to him and, seeing that the man was struck with wonder, asked him what the matter was. When he told him about the vision, the shrine-keeper asked him, 'Do you want to see if you can walk?' He said that he did and the shrine-keeper helped him up. And straightaway his sinews, which had become contracted through long disuse, rang out with a great sound as if they would snap when he stretched out his paralysed limbs. Unable to contain his astonishment or joy, the sick man burst out in praise of God, Our Saviour and St Richard, to whose merits he attributed this cure. They led him, accompanied by the praises of both clergy and people, to the High Altar and to the saint's tomb and, at the ninth hour, he got up and began to walk up and down without assistance. Moreover, his weeping sores began one after another to dry up and heal over and, cured both of the ulcerous fistula and of the original paralysis, he was restored to full health just as he had long desired.

Bishop Richard's fig garden at Tarring.

THE WINTER 'STAGE'

The image of a stagecoach ploughing through driving snow has become inextricably linked with Christmas because this is the way it has been regularly featured on Christmas cards since the nineteenth century. However, Arthur J. Rees in his book Old Sussex and her Diarists *tells us that Sussex roads in the past were a byword for muddiness and impassability – and not only in the depths of winter:*

Sussex must have been far worse off than the rest of England in this respect. In 1703 Charles, King of Spain, was six hours in travelling the last nine miles when on a visit to Petworth House. Defoe, in his *Tour through Great Britain*, published in 1724, describes an 'ancient lady' being drawn to church from her Sussex home, in her 'coach of six oxen.' 'Nor was it done in frolick or humour,' adds the author, 'but sheer necessity, the way being so stiff that no horses could go on it.' She was not the only Sussex resident who was thus conveyed to church. When Sir Herbert Springer resided at Brogle Place, in Ringmer, the roads into the parish were so bad that it was his custom to be carried to church in similar fashion – using eight oxen as compared with the lady's six. Judith, the widow of Sir Richard Shirley of Preston, directed in her will, dated 10 January 1728, that her body should be buried at Preston, 'if she should die at such time of the year as that the roads thereto were passable.' If they were not, she was to be buried where her executors thought fit. John Owen, who published a book called *The Traveller's Guide* in 1731, speaks of the roads of Sussex as deep and miry, and in many places in an

'The winter stagecoach in a snow-drift'.
(Illustration from *Coaching Days and Coaching Ways*)

impassable state. He advises the traveller upon them to break off the road, either to the right or to the left, to avoid the mud.

But there were other things beside mud. Frequent references by Owen and other writers to footpads and the gallows to be seen by the roadside indicate the dangers of road-travelling at the time. In 1731, only three high roads between London and the southern seaboard existed. One of these ran along the coast to Brighton (Brighthelmstone) and Newhaven, and from thence through Lewes to London; the coach passed three large gallows on the journey. The first of these was outside Lewes, the second within a mile of Croydon, and the third near Tooting. On these gallows a number of criminals, convicted at the assizes for various offences, were to be seen suspended.

Even earlier the state of Sussex roads was proverbial, 'Souseks full of dyrt and myre' is a line from a poem written in the time of Henry VIII, in whose reign was passed 'An Acte for amendynge of Highe Wayes in Sussex', already in a bad state of repair by reason of the heavy traffic to and from the iron mills of the Weald. But as the mills increased, the roads grew worse, and in the subsequent reign of Elizabeth another legislative measure was passed entitled 'An act for the preservacion in the Wildes of the Counties of Sussex, Surrey and Kent, and for the amendment of High Waies decaied by carriage to and from Yron Mylles there'; and the remedy proposed by the Act was to make the ironmasters repair them, which they did for a great many years. In 1696 the first Turnpike Act affecting Sussex was passed, though the collection of tolls by this means was adopted by the legislature thirty-three years before.

After the Sussex iron mills had gone, Sussex roads were still as bad as ever, but their badness was attributed to a different cause. Another early Road Act for the county, passed in 1709, attributes their state partly to the great traffic from all parts of Great Britain and foreign parts brought about by the curative fame of the waters of Tunbridge Wells – then just coming into renown. Another reason, according to the same Act, was the large amount of goods traffic constantly going and coming between seaports of the county and those of Kent, and the great number of oxen, sheep and other cattle travelling to and fro.

'Because of all this traffic,' the measure states, 'the said several ways have become in almost every place ruinous and impassable, insomuch that it is very dangerous to all persons, horses and cattle that pass those ways.'

Nearly fifty years later, Dr John Burton published an account of his travels into Sussex under the title *Iter Sussexiense*, which is a remarkable piece of work. Of his first sight of Sussex, seen from the heights, with the Sussex Downs looming picturesquely in the foreground, he has pleasant things to say, but not of its roads. 'For,' he says, 'I fell immediately upon all that was most bad, upon a land desolate and muddy, whether inhabited by men or beasts a stranger could not easily distinguish, and upon roads which were, to explain concisely what is most abominable, Sussexian. No one would imagine them to be intended for the people and the public, but rather the byways of individuals, or more truly the tracks of cattle drivers.'

Although public stagecoaches were introduced into Sussex in the seventeenth century, their advent was not enthusiastically welcomed by everyone, as testified by Robert Willis Blencowe Esq., editor of the seventeenth-century Journal of the Revd Giles Moore, Rector of Horstead Keynes from the year 1655 to 1679. *Blencowe provides an informative footnote (which he terms a 'remark') to a journal entry for the year 1676, in which the Revd Giles Moore, Rector of Horstead Keynes, travelled to London on business and on horseback accompanied by his manservant, and in which he recounts that 'Steph. Weller... lent mee his (horse) to ride to London, 2s.' and records his additional expenses as 'the chamberlaine 2s., the tapster, 3s 6d., ostler, 5s 10d.'*

The following is Blencowe's 'Remark number 79' from the Journal of the Revd Giles Moore, Rector of Horstead Keynes from the year 1655 to 1679:

The general mode of travelling in the days of Giles Moore was on horseback, and such indeed continued to be the case in the Weald of Sussex, from the wretched state of the roads, to a much later time. The 'steed' that 'would carry double when there's need' was an essential part of a clergyman's establishment, and if the wife went forth, she sat '*post equitem*' on a pillion. A change of habits in this respect, however, was just commencing, and coaches had been lately established, starting from London and traversing the kingdom, to the great disgust of those who were wedded to the old system of travelling upon horseback: and well may those who have enjoyed the pleasure of riding through a beautiful country in a fine day feel distaste for all other modes of travel. 'Will any man keep a horse for himself' asks a writer in those days, 'and another for his servant, all the year, for to ride one or two journeys, that at pleasure when he hath occasion can slip to any place where his business lies for two or three shillings, if within twenty miles of London, and so proportionally to any part of England? No. There is no man, unless some noble soul that seems to abhor being confined to so ignoble, base, and sordid a way of travelling as these coaches so oblige him to, and who prefers a public good before his own ease and advantage, that will breed or keep horses. Travelling in these coaches can neither prove advantageous to men's health or business, for what advantage is it to men's health to be called out of their beds into their coaches an hour before day in the morning, to be hurried in them from place to place till one, two or three hours within night, insomuch that sitting all day in the summer time, stifled with heat and choked with dust, or in the winter time, starving or freezing with cold, or choked with filthy fogs? They are often brought into their inns by torchlight, when it is too late to sit up to get a supper, and next morning they are forced into the coach so early that they can get no breakfast. What addition is this to men's health or business, to ride all day with strangers oftentimes sick, or with diseased persons or young children crying, to whose humours they are obliged to be subject, forced to bear with, and many times are poisoned with their nasty scents, and crippled by the crowd of the boxes and bundles. (*The Grand Concern of England Explained*, 1673)

As Sussex roads improved so the number of stagecoaches increased and competition became fierce. The following advertisement was regularly placed over the winter period by J. Tubb & Co. in the Sussex Journal *in the 1760s:*

This is to inform the PUBLICK
THAT on Monday the 29th Laft, the LEWES
MACHINE, to carry Four Paffengers only,
Will continue going from Lewes, during the Winter
Seafon twice a Week, viz Mondays and Fridays,
From the White Hart Inn in Lewes, by Uckfield, to
The Golden Crofs at Charing Crofs; and returns from
The above Golden Crofs Tuesdays and Saturdays,
The fame Way, to the White Hart Inn at Lewes afore
faid, Price Thirteen Shillings, as ufual each infide
Paffenger to be allowed fourteen Pounds Luggage,
All above to pay One Penny per Pound. Outfide
And Children in Lap Half Price. Sets out at Six in
The Morning. Performed by
J. Tubb and Co.

'Giving them a Start'. (Illustration from *Coaching Days and Coaching Ways*)

CROWBOROUGH AND UCKFIELD'S AIR-RAID SIREN PROBLEMS, CHRISTMAS 1939

From the Sussex and County Herald, *January 1940*

There have been periods in our history when the much-loved festival of Christmas has lost much of its joy and savour. Christmas 1939 is such an example, when the county was preparing for war and turning its mind to more pressing matters such as the safety of the civilian population. Over the Christmas period, Uckfield Rural Council met to discuss the inefficiency of its new air-raid siren. Despite the undoubted concern of the councillors, the report has something of the air of a scene from Dad's Army *as the Council, having mulled over the problem, end by taking the decision to do absolutely nothing:*

The clerk (Mr. Hadyn Thomas) reported that Inspector Mockford has brought him a letter from the Chief Constable as a sequel to complaints from a Crowborough resident regarding the siren. A map showed that on December 2nd the test revealed that it was heard in Jarvis Brook and district but part of the shopping centre did not hear it at all. In other parts it was medium.

Mr. Hadyn Thomas said in reply he pointed out that when the test was made the wind was West North West blowing towards Jarvis Brook. The Chief Constable had suggested the siren be moved from the Police Station to either Martins Garage or the Council offices. After consultation with the surveyor and the ARP Officer he found the cost of removal would be about £100. Even then it was quite possible that the next time the siren sounded the wind would be in an entirely different direction, and the audibility varied accordingly.

The Chairman (Mr. F.H. Nias) said that if the siren was removed it would require the engaging of three men for continuous duty. Mr. G. Watson said they had better sell the siren, and Mr. G.N. Martin asked if they were obliged to have a siren.

The Chairman said it was a funny thing that when the council wanted a siren at Crowborough and Uckfield it was turned down by the Home Office. Then they heard that the police must be in charge of the warnings, and immediately the Chief Constable took over, he told them they must have sirens at Crowborough and Uckfield. Now they had got them and they were not much good. In any case he did not think them much good in rural places because the first intimation of an air raid would be the firing of anti-aircraft guns.

Mr. C. Anley Hawes said when the siren was tested in Uckfield some of the people in the shops at the other end of the town did not hear at all. Mr. D Horscroft confirmed that statement.

Mr. J.R. Own said they did not know when sirens were going to be sounded, as sometimes when the enemy were over Britain sirens were not sounded. He thought they should not take action until forced to do so.

It was decided as far as the Council was concerned, that the siren should not be removed from its present position.

CHRISTMAS GHOST STORIES AND HAUNTINGS

Christmas seems to be the most prevalent time for haunting and Sussex is no exception. Traditionally solstitial times were those when the spirit world was believed to be most clearly connected to the real world and the twelve days of Christmas have been suggested to originate as a gap between the old Julian calendar and even earlier lunar calendars – a crack in time through which spirits could penetrate at this season. Certainly from Victorian times ghost stories have featured strongly as a part of Christmas entertainment, both in written and oral form. The setting for the reading of what is considered the most terrifying ghost story ever written – Henry James's macabre The Turn of the Screw *– is a Victorian Christmas house party, where the guests are telling ghost stories on Christmas Eve. James began the story whilst negotiating the lease for Lamb House in Rye, and finished it by December 1897, two months after signing the lease. James was himself told the story by the Archbishop of Canterbury at a house party at Addington. James's story begins with the reaction of the guests to a ghost story that has just finished:*

The story had held us, round the fire, sufficiently breathless, but except the obvious remark that it was gruesome, as on Christmas Eve in an old house a strange tale should essentially *be*, I remember no comment uttered till somebody happened to note it as the only case he had met in which such a visitation had fallen on a child. The case, I may mention, was that of an apparition in just such an old house as had gathered us for the occasion – an appearance, of a dreadful kind, to a little boy sleeping in the room with his mother and waking her up in the terror of it; waking her not to dissipate his dread and soothe him to sleep again, but to encounter also herself, before she had succeeded in doing so, the same sight that had shocked him. It was this observation that drew from Douglas – not immediately, but later in the evening – a reply that had the interesting consequence to which I call attention. Someone else told a story not particularly effective, which I saw he was not following. This I took for a sign that he had himself something to produce and that we should only have to wait. We waited in fact till two nights later; but that same evening, before we scattered, he brought out what was in his mind.

'I quite agree – in regard to Griffin's ghost, or whatever it was – that it's appearing first to the little boy, at so tender an age, adds a particular touch. But it's not the first occurrence of its charming kind that I know to have been concerned with a child. If the child gives the effect another turn of the screw, what do you say to two children -?'

'We say of course,' somebody exclaimed, 'that two children give two turns! Also that we want to hear about them.'

I can see Douglas there before the fire, to which he had got up to present his back, looking down at this converser with his hands in his pockets. 'Nobody but me, till now, has ever heard. It's quite too horrible.'

Unfortunately this superbly eerie tale is far too long to include in this anthology. Three Sussex Christmas ghost sightings are described below:

Patcham murder victim

Tony Wales in his *Sussex Ghosts and Legends* mentions a haunting highlighted in *The Sussex Weekly Advertiser* in 1796. The newspaper reported 'supernatural appearances which greatly alarmed some respectable persons' on Christmas Day each year outdoors at Patcham, on a spot where the remains of a murdered woman were subsequently found.

The Grey Lady of Patcham

Cecile Woodford mentions another Patcham haunting in her *Portrait of Sussex*. This was one experienced by her father as a young man in All Saints church. He attended a Christmas Eve service and saw a pale lady dressed in grey in a nearby pew who looked very cold. He spread his overcoat around her shoulders and she vanished during the singing of the final hymn, leaving his coat on the pew. He was sitting next to the door and did not see her leave. He was told locally that he had seen the Grey Lady of Patcham.

The De Braoses of Bramber

The thirteenth-century owner of Bramber Castle, William De Braose, occurred the enmity of King John – not a difficult thing to do! De Braose escaped to France, but his castle was seized and his family imprisoned. According to tradition his wife and family were starved to death and the ghosts of the children are sometimes encountered at Christmastime in Bramber, holding their hands out for food. If they are spoken to, the children disappear.

Bramber Castle from an engraving by Wenceslas Hollar

HASTINGS FISHERMEN'S CHRISTMAS CUSTOMS

The most picturesque part of Hastings is the Old Town, which is the fishermen's quarter. The fishing industry has undergone many changes since the first net-lofts were set up on the beach in the sixteenth century, but even today a crowd of distinctive black-tarred two- and three-storied lofts still house some of the fishermen's big nets and other gear on the beach, while the local fishing boats are still hauled up on the shingles as there is no natural harbour. The nearby Fishermen's Museum built in 1854 was originally the fishermen's chapel. We are beholden to Sandra Collins, Assistant Ship Keeper of The Fishermen's Museum, Rock-a-Nore Road, Hastings, for the following information on the fishermen's Christmas customs:

Hastings fishermen's huts under snow.

- The Winkle Club of Hastings was 'set up to help the poor fishermen and their families' and used their funds to organise an annual party for the children of fishermen, which was given on New Year's Day or as near to that festival as possible.
- One of the really exciting moments was when Father Christmas would arrive on the beach by fishing boat.
- The fishermen used to tie a Christmas tree to the foremast of their boats.
- Around 1940 a Mrs Terrell would arrange magic lantern shows for the children in the Wesleyan chapel in the Bourney, Hastings. The children would save a penny a week for twelve weeks and receive a Christmas stocking of sweets and fruit and maybe a small toy.

Father Christmas arrives on board the *Earl Brassey* in the late 1940s. (Photograph supplied by the Old Hastings Preservation Society) Ltd).

CHRISTMAS IN HASTINGS WORKHOUSE

'Workhouses for the poore' did exist in seventeenth-century England but they were very few and not unpleasant and an alternative to 'out-relief' paid to the poor in a parish. One early Sussex example was Old Lewes Poor House of St John sub-castro, Lewes; a flint stone house with a front of chalk blocks, standing on the north-west side of the Black Mount. In her article 'An Old Lewes Poor House' (Sussex County Magazine, *1928) Mrs Henry Dudeney quotes John Rowe who records that in 1633, 'the Lords of the Barony granted a parcel of land, lately part of the lord's waste, called the castle Banks, for the use of the poor. Upon this waste was built the house, and around it was planted a garden'.*

In 1834, the Poor Law Amendment Act was brought in to provide living-in accommodation for paupers and end all 'out-relief' for the able-bodied. Twenty-five parish workhouses (the 'Unions'), some of them enormous, were ultimately established in Sussex: in Arundel, Battle, Brighton, Chailey, Chichester, Cuckfield, Eastbourne, West Firle, East Grinstead, Hailsham, Hasting, Horsham, Lewes, Midhurst, Newhaven, Petworth, East Preston, Rye, Steyning, Sutton, Thakenham, Ticehurst, Uckfield, Westbourne and Westhampnett. Each new 'Union' was now managed by a locally elected Board of Guardians and they in their turn were responsible to the parishes they represented and to the central Poor Law Commission. Charles Dickens exposed the inherent cruelties of the early workhouse system in Oliver Twist *– the inhuman separation of families, poor food, a rough and easily identifiable workhouse uniform and, perhaps worst of all, deliberately degrading treatment.*

Initially the Commissioners ordained that no special Christmas fare should be served on Christmas Day and that only the medical officer could authorise any inmate to partake of alcohol on the premises. In 1847 the new Poor Law Board replaced the Poor Law Commissioners and charitably ordered that a full Christmas dinner (with all the trimmings) should be provided for the paupers, along with 'extras' (usually decoration of the communal halls and a Christmas tree) and that the inmates should do no work on that day other than that which was necessary for the cooking, serving and the cleanliness of the buildings. Throughout Victoria's and Edward VII's reign local dignitaries (with their families in tow) often chose to visit the workhouse on Christmas Day and eat Christmas dinner with the paupers – local newspaper accounts provided them with good PR coverage – often stressing how delicious and copious the dinners were as well as supplying interesting social details of any decoration and entertainment offered. One such example comes from

Hastings in 1814, by Owen after an engraving by F.W.L. Stockdale.

Hastings workhouse, reported in the local paper, The Hastings and St Leonards Pictorial Advertiser, *on 24 December 1908:*

WORKHOUSE EN FETE
GREAT TREAT FOR THE INMATES

Friday was a gala day for the inmates of the Hastings Workhouse. Thanks to the generosity of Mr. and Mrs. Harvey du Cros, every inmate was put into a state of joyful ecstasy by useful gifts and a musical treat.

During the afternoon, Mrs. Harvey du Cros, Miss Patricia and Mrs. Mossley, accompanied by Mrs. C.H. Ball, Mr. and Mrs. Harry Butler, Mrs. H.N. Cruttenden, Guardian J. Coleman and Mrs. Coleman, Guardian L. Watson and Mrs. Watson, Guardian Austin, Mrs. Oldrin, and Mrs. Andrews, toured the Union Infirmary, each inmate of the men's ward was presented with an ounce of tobacco and a clay pipe. Each of the old ladies received a quarter of a pound of sugar and two ounces of tea, whilst the youngsters were given toys of various kinds. Miss Patricia greatly enjoying herself in this ward.

The next scene of the treat was the dining room wherein a sumptuous repast had been provided for the inmates:

Then came the great event, a concert in the large dining room. On the walls thereof are hung specimens of the work of the inmates, many of which, particularly two paintings, were exceedingly cleverly done, and artistic withal. The hall had, moreover, been profusely decorated with Christmas greenery and bunting.

Mr. Baker Guy's Glee Party gave several vocal selections. Mr. Charles Fuller preceded with his usual skill at the piano. Mr. Anthony Collins, a clever young violinist, and Mr. W. Arthur Guy, an accomplished cellist, completed the orchestra. The audience was quick to appreciate the humour of Mr. Jack Cornelius, whilst chic Miss Madge Murray was also loudly applauded for her 'catchy' tunes.

At the conclusion a vote of thanks to Mr. and Mrs. Harvey du Cros and Miss Patricia was passed by the inmates with a gusto which showed how they appreciated the event.

Not all Christmases in the workhouses passed off happily or without incident. The following account is from the Hastings and St Leonard News, *January 1850, and reports an 'incident' which took place in the workhouse over the Christmas period 1849, and which resulted in a police conviction:*

CHRISTMAS FARE IN THE WORKHOUSE

Town Hall, Saturday, January 5. – Before Earl Waldegrave, and G. Scrivens and W.D. Lucas-Shadwell, Esqrs.

– Elizabeth Meek, 31, was charged with being guilty of misbehaviour in the Workhouse on the 31st of December, she being at the time an inmate.

The governor gave a brief outline of the case, and called M. Bumstead, who deposed – On the 31st of December, I was in the women's day-room with prisoner, Mrs. Quinnell, and others. Mrs. Meek brought in some pieces of plum pudding on a plate which she placed on a chair. A child of Mrs. Quinnell's endeavoured to take a piece and in doing so, threw the plate and pudding on the floor. Mrs. Meek slapped the child on its back. Mrs. Quinnell said she should not do that. Words arose. Mrs. Meek used bad language, and ultimately threw the largest piece of pudding in Mrs. Quinnell's face, who returned it to Mrs. Meek.

The pudding was thrown five or six times, when Mrs. Meek 'dabbed' it in Mrs. Quinnell's face. A fight ensued, Mrs. Meek getting Mrs. Quinnell down, tearing her cap off, and pulling her hair. One of the females went for the matron, who soon came out and stopped the fighting. Mrs. Meek struck first.

Harriet Clifton and Maria Ginner, two other paupers, corroborated the foregoing testimony. Prisoner made a statement, throwing the onus on Mrs. Quinnell. She stigmatised the witnesses as 'hypocryps', and complained loudly of the violent temper of the matron, who acted towards some of the paupers with great partiality, and was frequently in the habit of calling prisoner a 'dirty-gipsy' and a 'lazy wench', which later epithet contended, was exceedingly improper to apply to a married woman.

The Governor stated that he was not at all aware the matron used such language. He was desirous of putting a stop to such serious practices in the house, and would place Mrs. Quinnell before them, if the Bench thought fit.

The Magistrates consulted.

Earl Waldegrave (to prisoner) – 'The Bench have given your case the best consideration, and they order you to be imprisoned for fourteen days.'

Prisoner – 'Yes sir: I hope you will serve Mrs. Quinnell the same.'

On leaving the Hall, prisoner bowed to the witnesses and said 'Thank you, Mrs. Bumstead, I'll talk to you another day.'

Amusing as the account appears, it shows how the spoiling of such a small enjoyment could unleash in an institutionalised workhouse inmate all kinds of pent-up feelings that normally had to be held rigidly in check. Meek's biting comments on the matron, if true, indicate that the latter had little real respect for some of her charges (who were, after all, not prisoners, just poor widows, or spouses segregated from their husbands) and was controlling the paupers by means of sarcasm and stinging insults. A fortnight in goal for a slice of plum pudding seems harsh justice even if Meek was a consistent troublemaker – note her final rejoinder to Mrs Bumstead seems to carry a veiled threat. By emphasising Meek's misuse of the English language the reporter is poking fun at her as well as insinuating that Meek was an ignorant woman as well as a violent one, in addition to being a pauper – this was a combination which to the journalist, and perhaps to the majority of the paper's Victorian reading public, made her undeserving of sympathy.

By Act of Parliament, on 1 April 1930 all the Boards of Guardians who managed the Sussex workhouses (along with the other 609 Boards of Workhouse Guardians in parishes throughout England and Wales) were ordered to disband, and the Union buildings were sold off.

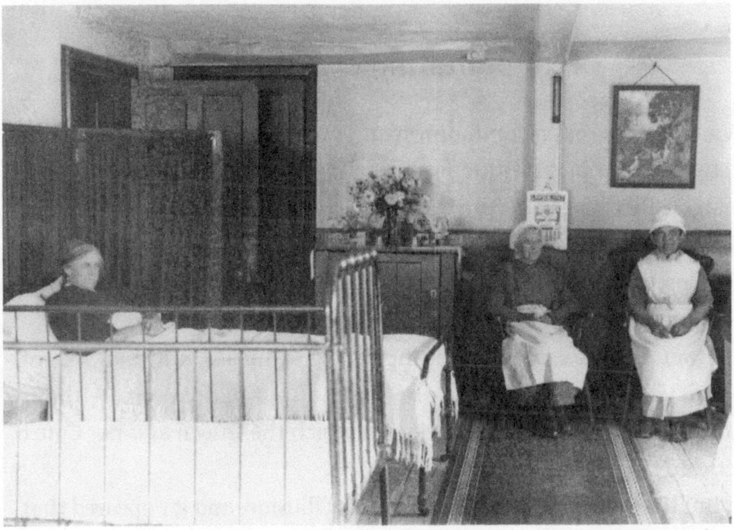

The women's ward at the workhouse, Petworth. (Copyright Garland Collection, West Sussex Record Office)

THE PUMPKIN RUM

By 'The Nomad' and 'Mrs Nomad', 1934

Pumpkins and pumpkin pie are usually associated with Hallowe'en, but this article and poem in the Sussex Daily News *describes a potent Christmas drink. In the article 'The Nomad' (pen-name of a regular columnist) meets the 'Pumpkin King of Lowheath' who teaches him the recipe for pumpkin rum and 'The Nomad' announces his intention of trying to make some. The disastrous consequences are described three months later in a poem by 'Mrs Nomad' in the Christmas issue:*

Pumpkin King of Lowheath

Wandering across a commonway at Lowheath, on the road between Petworth and picturesque Fittleworth, last evening, I came upon a man busily engaged in cutting and weighing some gigantic pumpkins. He was Mr James Pullen, who lives in a Sussex stone cottage facing the Downs in this glorious part of the country, and his activities were being performed on the common which adjoins his garden.

I had always associated pumpkins with fairies, and had a firm conviction in my mind that the shells of pumpkins were, without exception, converted into chariots in which the Queen and her Court rode on state occasions.

But the 'Pumpkin King' destroyed my illusion, and it appeared that there is more in this pumpkin question than meets the eye, however ludicrous it may seem at first.

But I will tell you all about it. From a twopenny packet of seed Mr Pullen has grown more than 20 pumpkins. He assured me that the combined weight of the eleven I saw him with last evening was more than 500lbs, and I can personally confirm that one monster, which he weighed while I was with him, turned his steelyard at nearly 90lbs.

Pies and Wine

In answer to my question as to the uses of these gourds, he informed me that they were made into pies, and wine, and he then explained how a very potent drink can be made from them.

It is done in this wise: You must scoop out the pitch in the middle of the pumpkin, being careful that you do not carry your hole right through so that it leaks, and then you fill up the cavity with moist sugar, and allow it to stand until the outside becomes quite soft. By this time the sugar will have eaten away the inside, and the gourd will be found to be filled with liquid. This liquid is carefully poured out, strained and bottled. I was assured that it made a very excellent and powerful refreshment! I am making a 'brew' in the pumpkin which 'The Pumpkin King' has given me. Mr Pullen assured me that his pumpkins had not been fed in any way, but that one was cut at Coates some years ago, which had been fed, and which weighed nearly 180lbs!

Method of Feeding

The method of feeding them is this: By means of a darning needle a piece of wool is drawn into the stem of the growing pumpkin, and the other end is placed into a bottle or jar of sugared water. The gourd will, I was assured, drink more than a bottle of milk a day, and take on added corpulence as a consequence ... And don't forget – my pumpkin brew will be ready soon. How soon I can't say but Christmas will be a happy time to try it.

The Pumpkin Rum Sequel by Mrs Nomad

O all you wives whose husbands dare
Suggest that pumpkin rum they make,
Come! Profit by my load of care
Which you'll agree did 'take the cake!'

For Mr Nomad learned a way
Of making good said pumpkin rum,
That lesson, I am sad to say
Was incomplete and lacking some!
'Tis true the recipe he followed
Of getting pumpkin 'first class grade',
And its inside having hollowed
With sugar filled the hole thus made.

So far – so good. He let it stay
For several days upon the shelf,
Then Sunday morn he said 'I may
As well with rum amuse myself.'

Amuse himself he surely did
With splashing here and splashing there,
He filled a jar up to the lid
And all the bottles we could spare.

Four bowls, two crocks, and things galore
With sticky rum quite soon were messed,
The kitchen ceiling and the door
Quite quickly ceased to look their best.

The recipe I fear did not
About the clearing up explain,
So Mr Nomad left the lot
To think of it brings on a pain!

My noble efforts all next day
Eventually got things straight,
Life flowed again on even way
Alas! Alack! How hard is fate.

On entering late one foggy night
Wanting nothing but my bed,
There fell upon my sleepy sight
A scene that made me see the red!

Something glistened on the floor
The place was full of trickling sounds,
Do I need to tell you more?
THE PUMPKIN RUM HAD BURST ITS BOUNDS.

The rum, the rum was everywhere,
You never saw quite such a sight,
The floor, the ceiling and the chair
With glistening drops of rum were bright.

T'was hours and hours, or so it seemed
Before the place was nice again,
And all the furniture redeemed –
The rum? It all went down the drain!

So all you folk who did intend
To call and sample pumpkin rum,
Though pleased we are to see a friend
The most we have is but a crumb!

The moral to this doleful tale
Is clear to ladies who may read,
NEVER let an erring male
Attempt this job – by this take heed.

James Pullen of Lowheath, near Petworth, weighing a pumpkin. (Courtesy of *Sussex Daily News*, 28 September 1934)

MIDWINTER STORM DESTRUCTION OF EASTBOURNE PIER AND THE BRIGHTON CHAIN PIER

Sussex is famous for its piers and infamous for its lack of care in maintaining them – witness the incredible catalogue of incompetence and neglect attending the demise of the Brighton West Pier. Two piers destroyed by midwinter storms in Victorian times – Eastbourne Pier and the Brighton Chain Pier – had their ends hastened by neglect. Only the Eastbourne Pier was rebuilt:

The Destruction of Eastbourne Pier, 1 January 1877
From the Eastbourne Herald

Looking out sea-ward, the scene presented was grandly wild, but at the same time gloomy and portentous; huge waves were seen rolling in, their white crests raised towards heaven, whilst the wind scattered the spray far and wide, forming a dense mist on the scene. It was a quarter past eleven. Huge crowds began to assemble and the sea continued to rise and advance with slow but steady step towards our shores the waves increased in size, breaking like mighty giants on the doomed pier and along the whole length of the parade.

The scene was magnificent in the extreme, quite baffling description; the waters rose up like an enormous wall, looking fearful in their power and descended with a blow which can only be compared to Vulcan's Hammer. The Pier began to stagger and violently oscillate and it became evident that it had completely broken in the centre. The excitement was now intense, as the first half, which was the weakest and received the greatest fury of the waves, gradually sank over to the east.

A few trusting and venturesome individuals believed it could yet resist the mighty power of the ocean, for they kept their places upon it. Old Neptune still raged, and boiled, and foamed with greater madness when, at a few minutes past twelve, a terrible crash was heard – a thrill of horror passed through the crowd – the Pier was gone. At first it was thought the men on the Pier had gone with it. But they saved their lives as if by a miracle, scrambling on to the falling floor by clinging to the railings, and being pulled upon terra firma by those at the entrance.

The Destruction of the Brighton Chain Pier, 4 December 1896
From the Brighton Herald, 5 December 1896, reprinted in Brighton Chain Pier *by John George Bishop, 1897*

The Brighton Chain Pier was destroyed in a storm last night. A very few words will suffice to tell of the last moments of a beautiful structure. It met its fate as everyone could have wished that it should meet it, at the hands of the winds and waves that it had for three quarters of a century so nobly defied. The end came about half past ten o'clock, or perhaps a few minutes later. A terrific storm of wind, with some rain, was then prevailing, as, indeed, it had prevailed earlier in the day, especially during the afternoon. These earlier attacks had evidently weakened the expiring strength of the structure, which at the head had already listed six feet out of the perpendicular, and when the storm recurred at night the hope that the Pier would last to daylight was virtually gone. Suddenly, amid the roaring of the waves and the howling of the wind, the Pier shivered convulsively from end to end; and in a few moments the entire structure had collapsed. Nothing remained standing but the vestiges of the first pile of timbers; and upon these the waves were thundering as though to make short work of the ruins. The sea was strewn with the great mass of wreckage, the huge weather-worn baulks of timber being seen, in the drifting rain and salt spray, riding like phantom boats upon the white crests of the waves.

The actual work of destruction was a matter of but a few seconds; but, so far as there was any difference of time, the light at the Pier-head was the last to disappear.

Though the fate of the Pier was expected, there were very few eye-witnesses of the final scene. One of them was Miss Body, who lives in one of the houses under the cliff, through which the suspension chains pass. About half past ten o'clock Miss Body was startled at a tremulous movement of the chains, which shook the house in a manner that they had never done before, and, in some alarm, she called out, 'What is the matter with the Pier?' and, going to the window, was just in time to sec the Pier collapse and the giant chains sink to the ground. To use Miss Body's words, 'All at once the light at the Pier-head disappeared, and in a moment the whole thing was demolished.' Pccring out of the window, a representative of the *Brighton Herald* saw all that was left of the Pier, – the shattered timbers of the first group of piles. Against the wall in front of the Aquarium the sea was bursting in great clouds of spray and foam, deluging the roadway, and bringing with it heaps of shingle and seaweed, whilst baulks of timber swept up from the beach by the force of the stormy sea encumbered the road. A little knot of spectators had gathered at the entrance to the Pier, risking the chance of the suspension chains falling still further and crushing them where they stood.

From another eye-witness of the final scene, Mr F.W. Wilson, son of Mr Councillor Wilson, we have an account of what happened as seen from another point of view, namely, from the Marine-parade immediately above the land end of the Pier. Mr Wilson and his father had gone down to the Front to see the storm, and were standing at the bottom of New Steine. At that time only about a couple of dozen persons were in the neighbourhood of the Pier. Suddenly a voice was heard in the darkness calling out, 'The old Pier is going.' Mr Wilson says, 'I looked in that direction, and saw the middle pile go; it fell in a heap. As it went, the chains sank and disappeared from our view. A moment or two afterwards there was a cracking as of breaking timber, and the tower of the first pile fell, as if dragged over by the weight of the chains and the span of the chains connecting it with the land sank right down.'

Down on the seashore at midnight last night great masses of broken weather-worn timbers strewed the beach. The fury of waves, as has been said, washed some of these heavy baulks on to the Aquarium-road. Others were carried to the westward, and were dashed with terrific force against the new Central Pier now in the course of construction opposite the Aquarium, smashing, so we are told, several of the iron screw piles, but the darkness of the night and the fury of the storm prevented any attempts from being made to verify the actual extent of the damage. It was, perhaps, a little working of the hand of fate that the Chain Pier in its last moments should strike a blow of some sort at the newer rival which indirectly in some measure had been the cause of its abandonment. Under the Central Pier a great heap of wreckage had been accumulated against the concrete groyne, forming a breakwater of logs nearly as high as the promenade, and so big that it broke the force of the waves. To the West Pier fragments of the now-vanished Pier were also carried by the waves, but the darkness prevented it from being seen whether any damage was done.

The Chain Pier had thus lasted a little more than seventy-three years. To one who had known it in the fullness of its symmetry and grace, beautiful in times of calm, and strong in times of storm, it was, indeed, a sorry experience to stand at midnight in the stress of the gale, with the salt spray dashing like the flick of a whip across one's face, and to see the white waves rolling unchecked (save for a few shattered timbers) across the space where the Pier had so long stood a thing of beauty, but now, in Coleridge's words, destroyed at last by:

The storms and overwhelming waves
That tumble on the surface of the Deep.

What remained of the demolished Pier the day after the storm presented a spectacle of the saddest character. At high tide but one pile (the first) stood in position – in mute companionship with the wrecked section of the Electric Railway contiguous to it – and a more melancholy picture could scarcely be imagined. The graceful pyramidical iron Towers which had stood upon it for so many years had been torn from their foundations and toppled over athwart each other, the suspension chains attached to them trailing listlessly down, speaking more eloquently than in words of their utter impotency – massive as they were – to resist the terrific forces which had overthrown them. At low tide the aspect of the ruins was even still more appalling. Out at sea little else could be seen of the erst beautiful structure but solitary fragments of timbers standing out from the foundations of the second pile, to the West of which was lying one of the fallen iron Towers, heavily rocked by the varying motion of the more modified turbulent waves which had overthrown it on the previous night. Farther to the South, one solitary piece of timber with shattered top alone indicated the situation of the third pile; while beyond that, where the more massive but still graceful portion of the structure which constituted the Pier-head had stood, there were but a dozen or so broken and naked poles standing out from the water to indicate its position; all else being either ruthlessly swept away by the waves or lying enshrouded beneath.

John Bishop's book quotes the following advert from a 'local journal' of 11 December 1896:

Wreckage from Chain Pier, Brighton

ON THE BEACH, opposite Albion Hotel
TO TIMBER & FIREWOOD DEALERS & OTHERS

Mr Thomas Chapman will Sell by Auction, on MONDAY, December 14th, 1896, at Twelve, 150 LOTS of USEFUL TIMBER, FIREWOOD, &c., relics of the late-lamented OLD CHAIN PIER.

Ticket issued to Brightonians in 1850 giving them free access to the Chain Pier.

A few timbers remain of the Chain Pier after the storm of 1896.

THE CHRISTMAS POSTMAN

The following article from the Lewes Churches Magazine *of 1868 takes us back to the good old days in Victorian Britain when the postman was respected and valued, and his services to the community highly appreciated. It is to be noted that though the handmade Valentine cards were immensely popular, the printed Christmas card, though 'invented' some years earlier, was expensive to produce and had not yet become popular:*

The Postman is a functionary of one of the marvels of civilisation, which has developed itself in the lifetime of most of our readers, and is still, year by year, making wonderful growth, and is expanding in new forms of usefulness; for the Post Office now not only circulates letters and newspapers, it has a vast business in Money Orders ... And has an enormous banking business, holding thousands of pounds for its depositors – it has also introduced a system of Life Assurances and Annuities, which, as it becomes known, will, no doubt, assume gigantic proportions; while to crown it all it will probably soon undertake the transmission of telegrams on a scale never dreamt of hitherto.

But these departments of the Postal Service ... have nothing to do with the work of the well-known character who is called 'The Postman', and who distributes with such marvellous regularity the letters and newspapers which day and night are being showered over our land in ever-increasing numbers.

We glean the following figures of the work done by 'The Postman' in this country:–

In 1839 there were delivered in the United Kingdom only 76,000,000 letters; in 1840, on the introduction of the Penny Postage, the numbers rose to 169,000,000, and this has steadily increased till the last Report gives the total number of letters delivered in the year as 597,277,616 or at the rate of 151 letters to each inhabited house, or of 28 letters to each person of the whole population.

And even this does not exhaust the work done for us by these useful public servants; they have delivered 940,771 packets ... [thousands of] samples ... And such un-letter like articles as ladies' jackets, nutmegs, candles, iron tubing, door handles, boots and shoes, cricket balls, opera glasses, small lamps, mousetraps, and many other articles.

'The Postman' has therefore ceased to be the sentimental personage whose knock was suggestive chiefly of the joys and sorrows of life as set forth in a popular song, which begins:

> What a wonderful man the postman is
> As he hastens from door to door,
> What a medley of news his hand contains
> For high, low, rich and poor,
> In many a face he joy can trace
> In as many a grief can see,
> As the doors fly open to his rat-tat
> And quick delivery,
> Every morn as sure as the clock
> Somebody hears the postman's knock.

Still, there is one day on which, in spite of the matter-of-fact innovations of the Sample Post, the letter-carrier's wallet still is redolent of sentiment and song – that is Valentine's Day. It appears that the number of Valentines posted in London was 542,000; that nearly one-fourth of these were posted in the western district, and also that the Valentines sent from London to the country were more than twice as numerous as those sent from the country to London.

The house-to-house delivery of letters is the principal item of expense to the Post Office. No-one would have thought that the cost of conveying a letter from the General Post Office in London to Barnet or to Edinburgh would have been practically the same, and yet such is the case, for the difference does not amount of one-ninth of a farthing.

As a class the letter carriers are a remarkably hard-working and trusty body of men, who are by no means high paid. It is thank-worthy that in the metropolis there are no deliveries whatsoever of letters on Sunday, so that the London Postman has the blessing of the day of rest, which is unfortunately denied to the letter-carriers in most country towns and in many rural districts.

The account clearly indicates that the postman in 1868 was not yet delivering the new-fangled Christmas cards promoted by Sir Henry Cole, director of the Victoria and Albert Museum.

'The Postman', c. 1868. (Illustration from a Lewes magazine)

LORD OF MISRULE AT CHICHESTER

From the records of Chichester Consistory Courts

During the Middle Ages a 'Lord of Misrule' was commonly elected in castles, monasteries and other communities to promote mirth and merriment during the Twelve Days of Christmas. They presided over bizarre activities in which order was inverted. The post and its traditions may owe something to the Roman feast of Saturnalia, where order and proprietary were also overturned and inverted.

The following brief account comes from the sixteenth-century records of Chichester Consistory Courts. On a cold winter's night on 30 December 1586, one William Brunne, an elected Lord of Misrule, was visiting his local inn, the Swan, when he came across a Mr Weston, a visitor to Chichester. Seeing an occasion for seasonal fun, Brunne exacted 'a fun penance' from Mr Weston, who was on official business from the Admiralty; and obliged him to submit to the indignity of riding a broomstick from the inn to the town cross at nine o'clock at night. The town cross at Chichester (built at the expense of Edward Story, Bishop of Chichester in 1500) is found at the junction of the four main streets in the city. An ornate stone octagonal building now without the cross which once surmounted it and gave the building its name, it was originally designed for the 'use and benefit of the poor', to afford them shelter and protection from sun and rain 'when they frequented the market'.

Mr H. Weston 4th day of March 1587 appeared and objected to the charge that he played at tables all night in an Inn in the city of

Chichester publicly to the slander of his function. He alleged that he was sent for by virtue of a Commission from my Lord Admiral to be examined about certain marine causes the 30th day of December last, and being in the town somewhat late so that he could not be dispatched to return home again the same night, he went to the sign of the Swan for lodging where being on the next day in the morning about eight of the clock he played at the tables with the good man of the house and he had not played above an hour's space but that one William Brunne who then played the part of a lord of misrule came in where this examinate was at play and said that that game was an Christmas game and so perforce took this examinate from thence and made him ride over a staff to the Cross.'

Chichester Cross in 1811, from an old engraving.

THE SINNER'S REDEMPTION

Sung by William Lemming of Terwick, collected by Clive Carey

Clive Carey collected many splendid West Sussex folksongs just before the First World War, including several carols. This one was collected in February 1911 from William Lemming of the village of Terwick; he had learned it from the tipteerers (mummers) at Brandean:

Let all that are to mirth inclined
Consider well and bear in mind,
What our great god for us hath done
In sending his beloved son.

Prepare and go, god's angel said
To Bethlehem; be not afraid,
And there you will find all on that morn
A blessed babe, sweet Jesus, born.

With thankful hearts and joyful minds
The shepherds went this babe to find,
And as the heavenly angels told
They did our saviour Christ behold.

'Let all that are to mirth inclined' by William Lemming, a carol learned from the tipteerers at Brandean.

That night, before the happy tide
A spotless virgin and her guide,
Who long was seeking up and down
To find some lodging in the town.

But mark how all things came to pass
The inns and lodgings fill-ed was,
That they could have no room at all
Except 'twas in an oxen stall.

That night the Virgin Mary mild
Was safe delivered of a child,
According unto Heaven's decree
Man, God our saviour for to be.

THE WINTERTIME COLLIER BOATS

From the Lewes Churches Magazine, *1866*

In these days of central heating it is too easy to forget the untold numbers of domestic rooms that were once heated by means of coal fires during the winter months.

One suspects that the following magazine article, dated December 1866, had its origins in a conscious-pricking sermon delivered on Boxing Day (traditionally a day on which Christians were encouraged to reflect on those less fortunate than oneself) and that it was later refashioned into a 'Christmas contribution' for the 1866 Christmas edition of the Lewes Churches Magazine. *It craftily targets its Victorian Sussex reader – cosily seated by a coal fire and reading the article at Christmastime – and informs them that the cosiness of their Christmas hearth could never be achieved without 'this black but comely comforter to our hearth' – neither could there be gas to light their houses or their streets:*

The subject therefore is – coal. The Sussex reader is then strongly urged to consider 'the toils and dangers' of the colliers working in the Northern coalfields – a world possibly as far removed from theirs as the planet Neptune – and also the keelmen – the men who labour to bring them their coal in the coal ships, also known as keelboats, in wintry conditions.

Thousands of men and boys (some are not eight or nine years old) do go to their daily work down shafts, and in these underground regions there are canals with boats bringing coal from distant workings and trains of wagons drawn by horses; these horses are let down the shaft slung in a net of ropes, and never come up again; yet they are sleek and fat, while the men and boys are mostly lean and pale.

The railways now convey a vast bulk of coal to London, but there are still about 8,000 ships of about 250 tons burden on an average, which are always employed by the coal trade ... they are all alike in having masts that are far from clean, sails that are far from white, and pumps that are frequently going, while they rarely come into port after their voyage to or from the North without a jib-boom gone or a railing or bulwark 'carried away' or some other mishap.

When 'in ballast' the collier is about the most unwieldy machine afloat, and rolls terribly in rough weather. When loaded, she is uncomfortably close to the water, and if there be much sea is most uncomfortably wet and unpleasantly dangerous, for there is no buoyancy in her, and instead of rising gently to the approaching wave, she plunges under it.

The captain, mate, three men, the apprentice and the 'boy', do not lead idle lives onboard the collier. There are fourteen sails to be hoisted, reefed, stowed, and hauled about, besides those set in light weather on booms projecting from the yards, and called studding sails. Under ordinary circumstances, nine out of the fourteen sails would be kept set during the night. The crew would be divided into two watches, one half being at rest.

Over these 200 miles [to the south] something like 5,000 coal ships are continually passing, and in addition, there are steamers and schooners from Scotland, Humber-keels engaged in the grain trade, timber ships from the Baltic, Dutchmen with oil-cake, Prussians with corn and fleets of luggers from the herring and mackerel fisheries. During the night, whether sailing or at anchor, all these vessels are bound to show lights; so it can be easily imagined how, in foggy weather, with sleet and snow, driven by a strong north-east wind into his eyes, the captain may mistake any one of these ship lights for some shore-light and so run his vessel aground; and the mistake becomes even more intelligible when it is borne in mind that the poor captain may have been on deck for a day and a night preceding with his vessel labouring under double-reefed topsails and the pump at work during every watch.

Whether we think of the landsmen or the seamen who provide us with coal, we see that they risk no little danger and bear no trifling discomfort in doing so; wherefore let us, as we gather around the cheerful fire, have a thought for the pale pitmen and their little 'Trappers' (the child colliers) in their subterranean darkness; and also for the hardy seamen in many a ship, and the 'boy' clinging to the rigging as the storm sweeps over it; and let our hearts say a prayer for them, while we thank God for His gift of the blazing coal. And praise him 'for his goodness and His wonderful works'. – Psalm cvii. 8.

'Colliers on Land and Sea'.

THE UP PARK ALARMIST

By H.G. Wells

H.G. Wells described Up Park as 'a handsome great house looking southward, with beech woods and bracken thickets to shelter the dappled deer of its wide undulating downland park'. The most famous owner of the great West Sussex mansion of Up Park was Sir Harry Fetherstonhaugh, who had an affair with Emma Hamilton (who danced naked on a table at Up Park) in his youth and then in old age caused a local sensation by marrying his dairymaid, Mary Ann Bullock. The span of Sir Harry's life combined with that of his wife (died 1875) and his sister-in-law (Frances, who inherited, died 1895) covered 141 years. H.G. Wells' mother became Miss Bullock's maid in 1850 and commented in her diary that at Christmas 'Up Park just did nothing but eat.' Wells' father became a gardener there in 1851 and the future Mrs Wells left to get married.

Margaret Meade-Fetherstonhaugh described Up Park during Mary Ann's widowhood: 'At Christmas time, tables of gifts were spread in the Great Hall, and within living memory, description of the piles of red flannel petticoats and mounds of red rounds of beef and Christmas pies and puddings have been lovingly retailed'.

When Frances Bullock, Sir Harry's sister-in-law, inherited Up Park she employed H.G. Wells' mother to be housekeeper. H.G. Wells wrote in his Experiment in Autobiography*:*

My mother became housekeeper at Up Park in 1880 ... Except that she was thoroughly honest, my mother was perhaps the worst

Up Park. (Photograph Geoff Doel)

Above left: Sarah Wells, H.G. Wells' mother, at Up Park. *Above Right*: A young H.G. Wells, c. 1876.

housekeeper that was ever thought of. She had never had the slightest experience in housekeeping. She did not know how to plan work, control servants, buy stores or economize in any way. She did not know clearly what was wanted upstairs. She could not even add up her accounts with assurance and kept them for me to do for her ... during my mother's thirteen years' sway at Up Park and thanks largely to the reliefs and opportunities that came to me through that brief interval of good fortune in her life, I had been able to do all sorts of things.

Frances took a Miss Sutherland to be her companion and Wells comments:

The place had a great effect on me; it retained a vitality that altogether overshadowed the ebbing tide of upstairs life, the two elderly ladies in the parlour following their shrunken routines.

Wells lived at Up Park in 1880/81 and at Christmas got snowed in and put on theatricals and wrote a newspaper:

A great snow storm snowed me up for nearly a fortnight and I produced a daily newspaper of a facetious character – *The Up Park Alarmist* – on what was properly kitchen paper – and gave a shadow play to the maids and others, in a miniature theatre I made in the Housekeeper's room.

HISTORY IN A HOUSE – ST MARY'S, BRAMBER

By Peter Thorogood

It was on a snowy winter's day in 1983 when Peter Thorogood, a world expert on Thomas Hood, poet, writer and pianist, and other members of his family came to view St Mary's, then empty, with a view to purchasing the 500-year-old property. This poem is both a celebration of the long and fascinating history of a beautiful and ancient Sussex house and a celebration of that first vision of St Mary's in the snow:

Like Wenceslas, with footprints strangely blessed,
Through Sussex lanes, by downland heights and coombs,
As pilgrims, then, had journeyed here to rest,
We came in snow to view the empty rooms...

Once Normans, Templars, Roundheads, Ranters came
(Memory has dimmed time's melancholy march) -
Now, thousands come to see the sturdy frame,
The dragon beam, the inglenook, the arch

Carved out with bishop's mitre, English rose;
The gilded leather, glowing in soft light;
The 'Painted Room' with fiery sea-scenes, shows
Some mystery of its past, still gives delight.

Think on these things: we stayed the errant minds
Of those who plied less positive pursuits
Than crimson hollyhock whose seedling winds
Through unrelenting stones to build strong roots.

The years have passed, the saving has been done -
Though joys, and sadnesses, have marked our days,
Our labours less, our vision all but won -
Time-honoured house, surpassing all our praise.

THE CHICHESTER BOY BISHOPS

The Bishop of Sussex heads a territorial unit of the Christian Church known as a see (or diocese) and has his palace and church at Chichester. Considered a successor to the Apostles, the Bishop is responsible for the good administration of his see as well as the spiritual welfare of those under his charge. For the great feasts of the Church, including the conferring of the priesthood, he wears the distinctive mitre and carries a crozier which is emblematic of his pastoral duties.

The first Bishop of Sussex was an Anglo-Saxon, Wilfrid, who built his monastery and cathedral on lands on the Selsey peninsula some time after 681. Bede tells us that Wilfrid's monastic lands were 'compassed by the waters on every side save the west where there remained a narrow strip of land'. Nothing now remains of those early buildings on the land-strip which were possibly eroded then engulfed by the sea but

Sussex legend has it that the bells of the old Anglo-Saxon cathedral ring out from under the waves on a winter's night. During the late eleventh century the Bishop's seat was transferred from Selsey to Chichester and in this post-Conquest period the great Romanesque cathedral with the Downs as a backdrop provided, as it does today, a striking landmark in West Sussex. This was not a monastic church and priests and canons serve the cathedral and Bishop whose palace and palace gardens are within the cathedral precincts.

During the thirteenth century a strange tradition arose among the choirboys in a number of cathedrals and parish churches; it was practised at Chichester and endured until the Reformation. On 6 December, the feast of St Nicholas, patron saint of children, one of the boy singers was chosen to become a 'Mock Bishop'. He was ceremonially dressed in scaled-down scarlet bishop's robes and given a mitre and miniature crozier and for a three-week period (until 'Childermass', the feast of the Holy Innocents, 28 December) was treated with mock respect as a 'pretend' Bishop, being led in procession through the crowded streets at Christmastime and 'presiding' over services which took place in the choir. Some 'boy bishops' even delivered a Christmas sermon. This could not have been effected without the full approval and connivance of the choirmaster and Bishop. It also demonstrates that the Christmas season was perceived in the medieval period as being a merry and light-hearted time, and that children were included in the fun. St Nicholas, on whose feast day the boy bishops were elected, was a fourth-century Bishop of Myra, and is the forerunner of our Santa Claus. His gift of gold to three poor girls as dowries is regarded as the forerunner of the Christmas present.

An item from the Chichester Cathedral accounts for 1534/35:

> Item for new makyng the robe of scarlet for the chyld boysshop to Lawrence 10d.

A CHURCH QUIRE VISITS THE GENTRY ON CHRISTMAS EVE, 1847

By Frederick Jones

Sussex parish quires in the Victorian and Edwardian eras were often invited (and expected) to give carol performances on Christmas Eve both at nearby great houses and at the local vicarage. They made their way there on foot, carrying their instruments, no matter how inclement the weather, and were usually given monetary remuneration as well as food and drink. Frederick Jones was a Sussex vicar's son and played the flute in the quire at Falmer church and these are his boyhood memories of the Falmer and Stanmer quires paying their annual Christmas Eve visits during the late 1840s. They are taken from an article he contributed to the Sussex County Magazine *in 1928; Mr Jones was then aged eighty-six and living in East Hoathly. The 'great house' mentioned is probably Stanmer Park:*

In old days, the choirs of Stanmer and Falmer combined at the festive time, and on Christmas Eve, at the Earl of Chichester's invitation, were marshalled in the Baronial Hall. With their violins, clarinets, bassoons, flutes and bass-viols, assembled in a circle before the burning Yule log, they sang the old time carols in a deep bass, led by fine tenors.

My memory goes back to the third Earl of Chichester with his beautiful Countess, the sister of the hero who led the Balaclava charge. In the intervals of the songs, the tall, handsome young ladies, with their brothers home from Eton and Cambridge, supplied the singers with cake and sparkling October ale as bright as sherry. It is difficult to say who had the greater pleasure, the hosts or the guests.

Receiving a generous gift at parting, the minstrels then came to the old rectory, my home, and there my father assisted in the carol singing, and the whole programme had to be sung through again. The carol 'See Seraphic Throngs' (harmonised by the rector of Buxted), was a special favourite, and was usually asked for. An anthem 'Arise', with a special bass solo, was another great favourite and was generally demanded.

'Christmas Eve'. (Illustration from a Lewes magazine, c. 1874)

MICHAEL TURNER'S EPITAPH

Michael Turner, one of the most famous and distinctive of the Sussex West Gallery musicians, wore a white smock frock with a red handkerchief, tie and breeches, plus a high beaver hat on Sundays. He was clerk and sexton of Warnham church for fifty years and died in December 1885, aged eighty-nine. The following verses are inscribed on his headstone:

His duty done, beneath this stone
Old Michael lies at rest.
His rustic rig, his song, his jig
Were ever of the best.

With nodding head the choir he led
That none should start too soon.
The second, too, he sang full true
His viol played the tune.

And when at last his age had passed
One hundred less eleven.
With faithful cling to fiddle string
He sang himself to heaven.

Michael Turner.
(Courtesy of Sussex Archaeological Society)

BRIGHTON PAVILION UNDER SNOW

The delightful and idiosyncratic royal residence known as Brighton Pavilion, with its onion domes, minarets and crocketed spires à la Indian Moghul, was an 1815-22 rebuild to the plans of John Nash of an elegant classical eighteenth-century house commissioned by George IV when he was Prince of Wales. The interior is no less arresting and exotic with its Chinese-style furnishings. The palace was regularly occupied by George IV, and also enjoyed by his brother William IV who succeeded him. Queen Victoria used it less regularly and ultimately sold it, but was thought to have much enjoyed her early visits. It appears that few Christmases were spent in the Pavilion – it being a royal tradition to spend Christmas at Windsor – we are however indebted to Andre Barlow, Keeper of the Royal Pavilion, for the following extract from the Sussex Weekly Advertiser *for 23 December 1816 which makes it clear that the Prince Regent was to spend Christmas in Brighton:*

> We have merely to observe that nearly three thousand persons were supplied with a sufficiency of meat and bread on Christmas Eve, for a good dinner on the following day...

A memoir of the Revd Edward Boys Ellman, the Sussex vicar, recalls in old age the year 1836, when he himself was a boy and enjoying Christmas with his family, when he claims King William IV spent a snowy Christmas at Brighton and invited certain worthies to attend his Christmas dinner:

That Christmas, 1836, was the one and only time that we were all together.

My eldest brother was at sea when my youngest brother was born, and was very little at home after that, his home-comings being few and far between; for it so happened that he had only two or three days' interval (not time to come home) before being gazetted to another ship.

On the evening of Christmas Day there commenced a very heavy fall of snow, which stopped all traffic in this part of England. The snow covered everything, and pathways in the roads had to be dug out. In one place, where a narrow passage through had been dug, the snow was considerably above my head on either side. Someone at Glynde Place – I forget who it was now, a visitor staying with the Hampdens – had an invitation to the Pavilion at Brighton, and offered a man ten shillings (more than a week's wages at that time) to take a letter to his Majesty. By avoiding the roads and keeping at a distance from the hedges, the man managed to wade through. He brought back word that no one else had reached Brighton from Lewes. The snow was not all melted for three months.

The west view of the Royal Pavilion, Brighton. (From Nash's *Views*)

King William IV entertains his guests in the banqueting hall at the Royal Pavilion, Brighton. (From Nash's *Views*)

Queen Victoria's last stay in Brighton, 1845. Prince Albert is driving the sleigh.

THE CHRIST CHILD IN SUSSEX

The Christmas crib and the forerunner to the Nativity play is claimed to be a creation of St Francis of Assisi (1181-1226). A preaching friar, he used real people and real animals displayed as a tableau vivant of the Nativity at Bethlehem so that his illiterate audience could better visualise the Christmas story. Apart from Mary's traditional blue dress and veil, there was no attempt to create an historical setting – his characters were dressed in their day-to-day contemporary clothes and the church itself provided a backdrop. We have two fascinating examples of an imaginative updating and relocation of the Christmas Nativity scene into the Sussex landscape. The first is in the church of St Michael and All Angels, Berwick, which is one of a line of Sussex churches (the others being Willingdon, Wilmington, Alfriston and Selmeston) built on ancient foundations on high ground.

During the Second World War, so many of Berwick's stained-glass windows were destroyed by bombs that the then Bishop decided to replace them with plain glass and to brighten the church with wall paintings. Duncan Grant, the eminent Bloomsbury painter, was elected to be responsible for the murals. At that time he and Vanessa Bell lived in the old farmhouse at Charleston near Firle Beacon, along with Vanessa's children Quentin and Angelica. Work was completed in their artist's studio by Christmas 1942 though the dedication service took place in the church in October the following year. Many of the Bloomsbury set had either been involved in the design and painting or sat as models. The Nativity scene, which is at the heart of the Christmas story, was set on the north wall and was painted by Vanessa Bell. Immediately striking is its contemporary Sussex setting. Though the mother and child are recognisably traditional they are displayed in a Sussex barn, and through the open door one can see Mount Caburn near Lewes set against a bright blue sky. Inside the barn are two shepherds dressed in rough twentieth-century clothes; they are carrying Pyecombe crooks and have brought a Southdown lamb as a gift to the Christ Child as well as a Sussex trug filled with eggs.

Our second example of a reconfigured and geographically relocated 'Sussex Nativity' comes from the book Saints in Sussex *(London, Cassell & Co., 1926) by Sheila Kaye-Smith (1887-1956). Kaye-Smith was born in St Leonards on Sea and as a married woman lived on a Sussex farm with her husband. A prolific writer, her* Saints in Sussex *is a compilation of poems and short plays dealing with some of the saints venerated throughout the liturgical year and in which Christmas is represented by a Nativity play entitled 'The Child Born at the Plough'. The play is set in four short scenes and 'the Plough' in this particular case is a Sussex public house.*

Kaye-Smith sets scene one outside a lambing hut on the marshes between Rye and Winchelsea, in the 1920s. Three 'lookers' (shepherds) in an exaggeratedly rural Sussex dialect are bemoaning the fact that they have been put out to lambing on Christmas Eve whereas they'd rather be in the Plough enjoying the Christmas beer. They sing the carol While Shepherds Watched *to while away the time and to celebrate the season; they are momentarily electrified when they are joined by the Angel of the Lord, 'dressed as a parson' but with a handsome pair of white wings sprouting from his shoulders. Informing them of the birth of a miraculous child at Udimore, he assures him that their sheep will be miraculously attended to while they visit the babe.*

Scene two takes place at the Plough, Udimore, where the landlady is serving a crowd of colourfully dressed gypsies. They are sympathetically discussing the latest local news – a woman has given birth to a child while sheltering overnight in the Plough's barn; the new mother and her elderly husband hoped to have been accommodated at the Plough but all the rooms had been taken. Unexpectedly Squire Herod and his second wife, a smart but aggressive American, enter accompanied by the wife's pretty daughter Salome, described as a 'tall flapper'.

> *Herod*: Get out of my way. Who are you to stop me?
> *David*: [with dignity] I am a king.

But being a 'king of the gypsies' does not impress Herod and the atmosphere becomes charged. Fortunately the Herods have to leave early – Salome is to dance at their dinner party and needs time to get ready. As the Squire storms out of the pub with his womenfolk in tow, he warns the landlady to expect trouble. Very important people are to dine with him that very evening – Mr Pilate the Mayor and Mr Caiaphas the Archdeacon – and they will be informed that there is a 'child in the stable'.

The landlady is shaken but, as Elijah the gypsy comfortingly comments, 'This ain't Caesarea, Idaho. It's Udimore, Sussex.'

The setting of scene three is the stable of the Plough – and highly reminiscent of the Vanessa Bell wall painting – Mary in a blue gown and with a shawl 'over her head and shoulders in the manner of the gypsies' is seated with the Christ Child in a high-roofed Sussex barn attended by Joseph, dressed in the clothes of 'a respectable artisan' of the 1920s. Tier by tier in the stable loft above their heads sits the Angel Choir singing the Introit of the Christmas Midnight Mass. One by one the gypsies then the shepherds and landlady do homage before the heavenly child. Scene four continues to bring a steady stream of unexpected people to the barn including John the blind beggar, Thomas à Becket, and three wise men from Cambridge who arrive by car. The Angel of the Lord warns Joseph to take the child and his mother and flee to Kent where they will be safe for a while. The following lines end the play:

> *Angel:* The dawn is here, though not yet the day. We have passed from midnight to Aurora. Lux fulgebit. Light shall shine to-day

upon us: for unto us the Lord is born. Fare you well. [With arm uplifted in salute he goes out through the open door.]

[Joseph goes up to Mary and puts his arm round her for a moment. He then returns to his old place on the further side of the manger, but this time he kneels. Mary kneels too, and for a minute they form the conventional group of the Christmas crib – Mary and Joseph and the young child lying in a manger. The daylight deepens as the Angel Choir sings the Communion of the Midnight Mass of Christmas.]

Angel Choir: The dew of Thy birth is of the womb of the morning.
[A cock crows]

Supporters of Sheila Kaye-Smith enjoy her religious zeal and find in her works a thoroughly convincing portrayal of Sussex people and the Sussex landscape, often comparing her works favourably to other regional writers such as Mary Webb and Thomas Hardy. One can certainly find in her work a social interest in that it mirrors the period in which she is writing, and suggests the language, prejudices, concerns and attitudes of a variety of social classes of the day.

Sussex shepherd, Soames Farm, Petworth. (Copyright Garland Collection, West Sussex Record Office)

THE CHRISTMAS HUNT

Although it was classed as vermin and of no food value, the red fox was long important to the hunting scene in Britain as a beast of chase. It has been hunted by hounds over the Christmas period since the Middle Ages, as indicated in the anonymous fourteenth-century poem Sir Gawain and the Green Knight, *which demonstrates that the fox's true interest as a quarry lies in its tenacity and guile as much as its speed.*

The following is an account of the Crawley and Horsham Christmas run which took place on 30 December 1905. Accepting that the Sussex countryside does not offer the flat, open countryside which is the ideal hunting country, the author writes:

Crawley and Horsham is a very difficult area to hunt requiring not only different hounds, but different horses for its varying features. There is the forest, with heather and bracken; large coverts so close together as to make a woodland country; the open Weald where hounds and horses need pace and the latter should be good jumpers, and finally, the Downs where the small bitches alone do not get tired and where a well-bred galloper is required. A short-legged stocky mount is best in the forest country...

A splendid day followed the meet at Abingworth, Thakeham. Finding at Bacons Land, the dog pack ran through Warminghurst Gorse, Hooklands, Perrylands, Lodge Copse, Frenchlands and Hawking Sopers to Guesses. Leaving Birch Copse on the right, they went on through Copyhold to Chanctonbury Ring, along to Steyning rifle butts and on to just north of Cissbury. Turning northwards, the fox ran to Highden and down the hill to Sullington and through Sandgate to

Warminghurst Church. Turning left-handed, he went by Strawberry Lane to Roundabouts and was finally killed at Smock Alley ... The point from the find to Steyning Hill was six miles and thence to the kill, seven. The hunt was 24 miles as hounds ran and the time 2 hours 40 minutes without a check until Warminghurst Church had been reached.

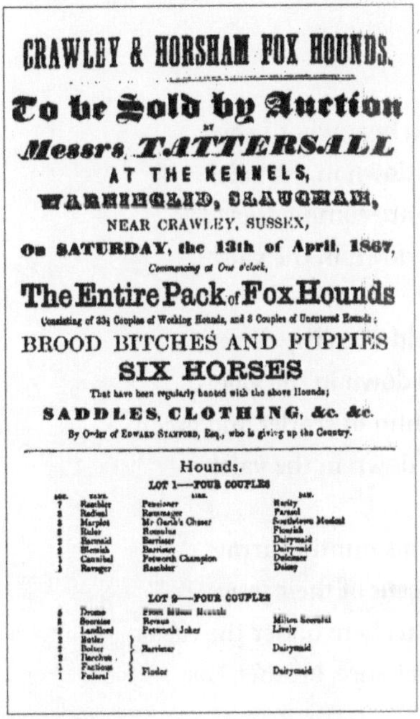

CRAWLEY & HORSHAM FOX HOUNDS.

To be Sold by Auction

BY

Messrs. TATTERSALL

AT THE KENNELS,

WARNINGLID, SLAUGHAM,

NEAR CRAWLEY, SUSSEX,

On SATURDAY, the 13th of April, 1867,

Commencing at One o'clock,

The Entire Pack of Fox Hounds

Consisting of 33½ Couples of Working Hounds, and 8 Couples of Unentered Hounds;

BROOD BITCHES AND PUPPIES

SIX HORSES

That have been regularly hunted with the above Hounds;

SADDLES, CLOTHING, &c. &c.

By Order of Edward Stanford, Esq., who is giving up the Country.

Hounds.

LOT 1—FOUR COUPLES

AGE.	NAME.	SIRE.	DAM.
7	Rambler	Pensioner	Rarity
3	Radical	Rummager	Parasol
3	Marplot	Mr Garth's Chaser	Southdown Medal
3	Ruler	Romulus	Flourish
2	Barmaid	Barrister	Dairymaid
2	Blemish	Barrister	Dairymaid
1	Cannibal	Petworth Champion	Dulcimer
1	Ravager	Rambler	Daisy

LOT 2—FOUR COUPLES

AGE.	NAME.	SIRE.	DAM.
6	Drome	From Milton Hounds	
3	Socrates	Reveus	Milton Scornful
3	Landlord	Petworth Joker	Lively
2	Butler	Barrister	Dairymaid
2	Bolter	Barrister	Dairymaid
2	Bacchus	Barrister	Dairymaid
1	Factious	Finder	Dairymaid
1	Federal	Finder	Dairymaid

Notice of sale of an entire pack of fox hounds, 1867.

'The Song of the Foxes'. (Illustration from a Lewes magazine, c.1874)

THE SONG OF THE FOXES

From the Lewes Churches Magazine, *Vol. IX, 1874*

Young Fox:

Ho! Brother Fox, dost thou hear what I say?
Hey for the coppice-wood down in the vale!
The hunt and the hounds are coming this way.
Hey for the coppice-wood down in the vale!

The master, I know him, old Timothy Sheen,
Hey, for the coppice-wood down in the vale!
And the field that is with him in scarlet and green,
Hey for the coppice-wood down in the vale!

I've seen him just now, in his hunting array;
His dogs all bout, on the scent of their prey.
Now should they but find us here under the rocks,
I'd give but a song for our chance, brother Fox.

Old Fox:

Why then, if they're coming, we'd best make away,
And leave them to find such sport as they may.
And if they've a mind to be riding all day,
It doesn't hurt us, let them have their own way.

SUSSEX MUMMERS AND TIPTEERERS

'Tipteerers' is a Sussex term, defined in the Revd William Parish's 1875 Dictionary of the Sussex Dialect *as 'Mummers who go round performing a sort of short play at Christmas time'. Mummers performed traditional plays at midwinter in many areas of England and hundreds of texts or fragments survive and have clearly developed through oral tradition with recognisable eighteenth- and nineteenth-century topical allusions added in. Their origins are controversial: some have suggested affinity with European pre-Christian ritual drama with seasonal, death and resurrection, sympathetic magic and disguise elements dominant; others have suggested an eighteenth-century origin commensurate with the first recorded performances and parts of texts (though this fails to explain why the parts are traditionally taken by men). To anyone with knowledge of the development of the English language and in particular dramatic forms, the texts, or their origin, in part clearly go back at least to the mid-sixteenth century and the crusading ethos could take us back even earlier.*

Records of dozens of Sussex teams and nearly as many plays survive in Sussex, with the villages around Chichester and Midhurst forming a

Chithurst mummers, c. 1911.

particularly strong tradition. The earliest account of a team of mummers in Sussex is in the Chichester area and confirms that, as in Thomas Hardy's Dorset, the actors were mainly young lads. This sad account of the inquest of a dead mummer from the Hampshire Telegraph *of 31 December 1821 (kindly supplied to us by the Chichester Museum) shows the effect of excessive alcohol from the night's entertainment on a thirteen-year-old:*

> MELANCHOLY CIRCUMSTANCE WIHCH TOOK PLACE IN SUSSEX ON 29 DECEMBER
>
> A party of youths with a view of keeping up an old custom denominated Tip Teering sallied from Chichester on Monday evening and pursued the route of Hampnett, Westhampnett, Welberton (Walberton) and Goodwood and having finished their tuneful sound they agreed in order to counteract the effects of the cold to run home, when Richard Cooper aged 13 years who was hindmost, having fallen in a ploughed field was left behind. On a search being made a short time afterward he was discovered lifeless in a field at Woodend. The extra beverage which he had taken combined with the cold and damp situation in which he fell caused his death. VERDICT – Died from the inclemency of the weather.

Chanctonbury mummers at Steyning, 1973. (Photograph Geoff Doel)

THE COMPTON TIPTEERERS

From The Wonderful Weald *by Arthur Beckett, 1911*

By the time that Arthur Beckett saw the Compton mummers' play in 1911, photographed it and took down the text, the play was clearly being performed because it was a well-established practice which gave social enjoyment and some benefit in money, food and drink. Beckett's reference to a tipteerers' play being performed in the kitchen of Richard Cobden's new stately home, Dunford House (constructed around a core of the farmhouse which had been his birthplace) in the 1860s, is interesting in this context. By 1911 traditional customs and songs were already in decline amongst the rural working classes (themselves a diminishing sector), but fortunately the customs (including the mummers' plays) and the songs were being collected and researched. So although the First World War virtually ended the traditional performances of plays by village communities through oral transmission, the wealth of revivals by groups such as the Boxgrove Tipteers (a touring group using amalgams of traditional West Sussex texts) and the Ditchling Players between the wars and by Morris sides (notably Chanctonbury and Ditchling) and folk clubs (notably Lewes) after the Second World War has meant that scarcely a year went by in the twentieth century without the performance of a Christmas mummers' play in Sussex, possibly a unique situation amongst counties.

Arthur Beckett's account of the Compton play is a classic in its observation of ethos and detail:

Divertisement – which tells of the Tipteerers

Among the many pleasant and delectable things of old-time Sussex there was ... a certain play or mummery, the which it was a custom to perform at the season of Christmas. This play was a rustic play, being given by villages. It was, moreover, not only ancient but curious. Also, so far as I could gather, it had not any special title; but in west Sussex the players called themselves 'Tipteerers'.

I had once seen this play or mummery given when I was a boy. ... Some years later I met another band of Tipteerers in a village near Worthing ... I am informed by Mr T. Fisher Unwin that an annual performance of the Tipteerers Play has been given every Christmas for the last six or seven years by schoolboys at Mrs Fisher Unwin's country house at Heyshott (Richard Cobden's birthplace). Mrs Unwin remembers the villagers performing the play in the kitchen at 'Dunford' at Christmas in the sixties. It was also given in Lodsworth village about the same time.

Beckett's description of the Compton Tipteerers follows:

There presently came into the vicarage drive a number of young men and boys fantastically arrayed; and counting them I found that there were seven, all curiously dressed but one, who had not attempted to disguise his modern clothes. But he was not the least important personage, for he carried an accordion to play upon during the march, and a cow's horn by which he announced the coming of the Tipteerers to outlying farms and houses; also his was the hat that took largesse from the spectators such time as the play was brought to its conclusion.

Of the characters of the play I learned that these, in such sort, were named Father Christmas, St George, the Valiant Soldier, Little Johnny

The Compton Tipteerers. (From Arthur Beckett's *The Wonderful Weald*)

Jack, the Doctor and the Turk. There should have been another representing Beelzebub, but for some reason or another he did not appear, and his part was therefore taken by Father Christmas ... Father Christmas wore an old top hat in which was a pheasant's wing and a bunch of mistletoe; his face was blacked (and in this matter of blacking the features he followed the custom that I had previously observed in other rustics who played his part); his long beard was of horsehair. He wore a long frock-coat ... The heathen Turk wore a policeman's or soldier's helmet (the back part turned to the front) decorated with rags of many colours. Strips of coloured rags also covered his clothes; and similar decorations were worn by the other players, some having cut out pieces of tinted cloth to represent quaint animals and figures, and some wearing a high head-gear in which they had stuck pheasant's tail feathers. Wooden staves represented swords and spears ... The actors themselves were the village smith and certain farm labourers, and each had his trousers braced high above the tops of his heavy soled boots.

The Compton Tipteerers told me that the words of their play had never been written down, but that they themselves had learnt them from predecessors, and thus the play had been handed down for hundreds of years. I had some little difficulty in persuading these good fellows to commit their mummery to writing, for no single man knew the parts of his fellows; and when at length the written words were delivered to me I found the speeches strangely jumbled, rhyming lines being written as prose, no indication of the character speaking being given.

I shall ... give you the play as I disentangled it from the pencilled ms which ultimately came to me, correcting only certain spellings, but preserving the words as they were spoke.

Despite Arthur Beckett's final comment, Old Father Christmas did double as Beelzebub at short notice in the performance he witnessed and presumably knew the lines:

The Compton Tipteerers Play

Valiant Soldier:

In come I, a roamer, a gallant roamer,
Give me room to rhyme,
I've come to show you British sport
Upon this Christmas time.
Stir up your fire and give us a light,
And see the merry actors fight.
For in this room there shall be shown

The heaviest battle ever known,
Betwixt St George and the Turkish Knight.
If you don't mind to believe these few words I've got to say,
Let the old Gentleman of all slip in and clear the way.

St George:

In come I, St George, that man of honour and courage, stout and bold;
With my sword and spear all by my side I have won twelve crowns of gold.
It was I who fought the Fiery Dragon and brought him to great slaughter,
And by those means I hope to win the King of Egypt's oldest daughter.

Valiant Soldier:

In come I, a soldier stout and bold;
As I was walking along the road
I heard great wonders and talks of you, St George;
If I was to meet thee I would prick thee through and through,
And make thy precious blood to flow.
Come in, thou Turkish Knight,
While we are here to-night
We are not to bear the blame.

Turkish Knight:

In come I, the Turkish Knight,
Just come from Turkey-land to fight.
I'll fight thee, St George – that man of honour, courage, stout and bold,
Let not his blood be ever so hot I will quickly make it cold.

St George [aside]:

Dare say you would, too!
Stand back, stand back, you noble Turk, or by my sword you'll die,
I'll cut your giblets through and through, and make your buttons fly.

Turkish Knight:

Pardon me, St George, pardon me I crave.
And ever more will I be thy Turkish slave.

St George:

You saucy little rascal! Ask me to spare your life after being so confounded bold! Been up in my best room, and stole my best clothes! Not only that, but took a watch from my pocket. I'll up with my sword and run thee through and through.
[Does so, Turk falls]
[To Father Christmas]

Behold, old man, and see what I have done,
I've cut your noble champion down just like the evening sun.

Father Christmas:

Seems as if you have done it now.

St George:

Well Father, what was I to do? He gave me the challenge three or four times and why should I deny?

Father Christmas:

Go home, you saucy rascal! Behold, yea, is there a doctor to be found?

The Doctor [coming forward]:

Yes, old gentleman, there is a doctor to be found
Who can quickly rise your poor son who lies bleeding on the ground.

Father Christmas:

Do you call yourself a doctor?

The Doctor:

Yes, old gentleman, I am a doctor.

Father Christmas:

You come in more like three-ha'porth o' bad luck than you do a doctor.

The Doctor:

Don't matter what I come in like, or what I look like, as long as I can rise your poor son who lies bleeding on the ground.

Father Christmas:

I don't know as you can do it yet. What is your pay?

The Doctor:

Ten pound is my pay;
Full fifty I'll have out of you before you go away,
You not being a poor man.

Father Christmas:

I can't pay so much money as that;
I'd sooner let him lay there and die.

The Doctor:

Stop, old gentleman, I'll satisfy you with quarter-part o' that.

Father Christmas:

That's according to what you can cure.

The Doctor:

I can cure all sorts of diseases:
The itch, the stick, the palsy, the gout,
Raging pains within and without.
This young man's arm's broke, his leg's broke,
Calf swollen up as big as a tan-leather bottle.

Father Christmas:

As big as a wooden-legged bottle, more like it.

The Doctor:

Rec'lect, old gentleman, I ain't been about all my time a-life without knowing nothing.

Father Christmas:

Where did you get all your learning from?

The Doctor:

I travelled for it: I travelled France, 'Merica, Spain and Dover,
I travelled the wide world all over.
I served my 'prenticeship in St John's Hospital seven year all one summer.

Father Christmas:

Seven year all one winter, more like it.

The Doctor:

I could rise this young man before your face. So could you if you know'd how and which way. So I did and so I can. I rose my poor old grandmother after she had been dead a hundred and ninety-nine years. She cut her throat with a ball o' rice; I slipt in and sewed it up with a rice-chain.

Father Christmas:

Talk about what you run-about doctors can do!

The Doctor:

Look here, old gentleman. I had a man brought to me the other day; indeed, he was not brought to me, he was wheeled to me in a left-handed wheel-barrow. He could not see anything without opening his eyes, and could not speak without moving his tongue.

Father Christmas [aside]:

(No) more would you,
Or else you would not talk so fast as you do.

The Doctor:

Look about, old gentleman, another curious trick I'll show you before I go away. Look deedy, or else you won't see it kick, and troublesome cure yourself for me.
[Going]

Father Christmas:

Stop, doctor, stop! Come and try one of your pills on my poor son, sooner than having him lying about here all this Christmas.

The Doctor:

I've got a little bottle in my waistcoat trouser breeches pocket, what they call okum, slokum, elegant plaint. I don't.

Father Christmas:

What do you call it?

The Doctor:

That makes no difference, so long as you drop
One drop on the young man's heart and another on his brain,
He will rise and fight bold Champion again.
[Doctor proceeds to cure Turk]

Turkish Knight:

How long have I been lying on this floor?
Ten minutes or more,
I've been urged and scourged and dragged from door to door.
To-morrow morning at the hour of five,
I'll meet thee, St George, if I am alive.

St George:

To-morrow morning, at the hour of ten,
I'll meet thee spring guard, with fifty thousand men.
I'll hage thee, gage thee, and let thee know
That I am St George over old England.
Go home, go home, you Turkish Knight,
Go home to your country and fight;
And tell those 'Mericans what I've done;
I've killed ten thousand to thy one.
Now I am off (to) my discharge.
God bless the Turk, likewise St George.

Johnny Jack:

In come I, little Johnny Jack,
Wife and family at my back.
Though I am so little and small
I am the biggest rogue among you all.
If any man offend me I bring him to a stand.
Cutter and Slasher is my name,
From those blessed wars I came.
It was only me and seven more
Fought the battle of a score,
And boarded a man-of-war.
Cut them up as fine as any flying dust,
Send them to cook-shop to make mince-pie crust.

St George:

What little rattling, prattling tongue is that I hear?

Johnny Jack:

That's mine, sir.

St George:

If I hear any more of that, you and me will have a cut before we part
On my heart, before we part.

Turkish Knight:

In come I, Cuts and Scars,
Just returning from those wars.
Many a battle I've been in,
Many a battle I have seen.
I've seen St George and all his royal men.

Cannon ball passed by my head with spite –
I lost my height.
Twice through the head I've been shot,
Which makes my brain boil like my old pot.
What more can be bolder?
Enter in the Valiant Soldier.

Valiant Soldier:
In come I, a Valiant Soldier, Bold and Slasher is my name,
With my sword and spear all by my side I hope to win this game.
Now I am a soldier stout and bold,
I make many a man's blood run cold.
Now I am returning from those wars,
I am a man like you, full of cuts and scars.
Pull out your sword and fight, pull out your purse and pay,
Satisfaction I will have before I go away.

Turkish Knight:
No satisfaction will I give thee, no more will I pay,
But this battle we will fight both manfully before we go away.

They fight and are separated by Johnny Jack, alias Twin-Twan:

Johnny Jack (as Twin-Twan):
In come I, Twin-Twan,
The left hand of this press-gang;
I pressed all these bold mummers sin'
The time the ship-of-war came in.
Although my name is Saucy Jack,
Wife and family at my back,

Out of eight I've got but five,
And they are almost starved alive.
Some in the workhouse all alone,
And these at my back must be helped before I get home.
So if any man would like to fight let him come on;
I urge him, scourge him, fight him with spite,
And after that I fight the best man under the sky.

Father Christmas:

You saucy little rascal! Challenge your poor old father and all the sons he's got?

Johnny Jack:

Yes; I urge him, scourge him, fight him with spite,
And after that I fight the best man under the sky.

Beelzebub:

In come I, old Belsey Bob,
On my shoulders I carry my nob,
In my hand a dripping pan,
Don't you think I'm a funny old man?
Christmas comes but once a year,
And likes to give you jolly good cheer;
Plum-pudding, roast beef – who likes that better than anybody else?
To-night I'd like a glass of grog; a glass of beer'll suit these chaps to-night.
Price, sir! Price, sir! Give you a bit of a rub?
A halfpenny towards the rent, and a penny towards the grub.
Price, sir! Price sir! And my old bell shall ring,
Put what you like in my old hat and then these chaps will sing.

Immediately the Tipteerers joined in singing the mummers' carol:

As we come out on a Christmas Day,
Christmas Day, Christmas Day,
As we come out on a Christmas Day,
So early in the morning.

We saw three ships come sailing by,
Come sailing by, come sailing by,
We saw three ships come sailing by,
On Christmas Day in the morning.

And who should be in those three ships,
Those three ships, those three ships?
And who should be in those three ships?
'Twas Joseph and his Fair Lady.

He did whistle and she did sing,
And all the bells on earth did ring,
For Christ our Saviour he was born,
On Christmas Day in the morning.

Jack was nimble and Jack was quick,
Jack jumped over the candlestick,
Jack was nimble and Jack was quick,
On Christmas Day in the morning.

Without a pause the Tipteerers, changing the air, gave another carol:

Brave Joseph and Mary to Bethlehem was bound,
They travelled to they was weary and no lodging they found,

In the city of David where they did overhall,
No place could they find there but in an ox stall;
This place was not so braved as Mary might be,
'Tis the birth of our Saviour, the King of Glory.
Many angels was assembling and the clouds did appear,
The shepherds stood a-trembling and smited with fear:
'Fear not,' said he, 'tis be not afraid,
'Tis a salutation to the people,' he said.
Be no longer a stranger in this world swaddle in close,
They laid him in a manger till the shepherds arose:
To save and redeem from the guilt of our sin,
My faith we lead us a new life again.
To remember our Saviour he was kind to the poor,
Its no more than a reason and a blessing in store.

Finally the Tipteers, having duly received largesse, sang their blessing:

The Compton Tipteerers carol

God bless the Master of this house
And send him long to reign,
And many a Merry Christmas
May he live to see again.
God bless the Mistress of this house
With a gold chain round her neck,
Where ever her body wakes or sleep,
God send her soul to rest.

God bless your house and your cattle,
To your family all in store,

May the Lord increase you day by day
And send you more and more.

My song is sang and I must be gone,
No longer canst stay here,
So God bless you all both great and small
And send you a happy New Year.

The Compton Tipteerers. (From Arthur Beckett's *The Wonderful Weald*)

CHRISTMAS AT COLD COMFORT FARM

By Stella Gibbons

Many readers will be familiar with Stella Gibbons' (1902-89) first highly successful novel, the brilliant satire Cold Comfort Farm *(1932) which won a prestigious Prix Femina Vie Heureuse literary prize in 1933. This hugely funny novel deals with the dysfunctional Starkadder family who live on an isolated, horrendously dilapidated farm in Sussex and whose members are either prone to extravagant emotional scenes and bizarre mannerisms or display truly disturbing religious fanaticism. One by one they undergo a metamorphosis through the determined efforts of their indefatigable young relative, Flora Poste.*

Christmas at Cold Comfort Farm *post-dates the novel and was originally written for the 1938 Christmas edition of* The Bystander. *Once again Gibbons gives us a brilliant parody of the primitivist novel genre popularised by such writers as Sheila Kaye-Smith among others, and once again sets the scene in Sussex where the near-insane members of Cold Comfort Farm are celebrating Christmas – before the advent of Flora:*

It was Christmas Eve. Dusk, a filthy mantle, lay over Sussex, when the Reverend Silas Hearsay, Vicar of Howling set out to pay his yearly visit to Cold Comfort Farm...

The Starkadders, of Cold Comfort Farm, had never got the hang of Christmas, somehow, and on Boxing Day there was always a run on the Howling Pharmacy for lint, bandages, and boracic powder. So the Vicar was going up there, as he did every year, to show them the ropes a bit...

The farmhouse was in silence and darkness. He pulled the ancient hell-bell (once used to warn excommunicated persons to stay away from Divine Service) hanging outside the front door, and waited.

For a goodish bit nothing happened. Suddenly a window far above his head was flung open and a voice wailed into the twilight:-

'No! No! No!'

And the window slammed shut again.

'You're making a mistake, I'm sure,' shouted the Vicar, peering up into the webby thongs of the darkness. 'It's me. The Rev. Silas Hearsay.'

There was a pause. Then -

'Beant you postman?' Asked the voice, rather embarrassed.

'No, no, of course not; come, come!' Laughed the Vicar, grinding his teeth.

'I be comin', retorted the voice. 'Thought it were postman after his Christmas Box.' The window slammed again. After a very long time indeed the door suddenly opened and there stood Adam Lambsbreath, oldest of the farm servants, peering up at the Reverend Hearsay by the light of a lonely rushdip (so called because you dipped it in grease and rushed to wherever you were going before it went out).

'Is anyone at home? May I enter?' Enquired the Vicar, entering, and staring scornfully round the desolate kitchen, at the dead blue ashes in the grate, the thick dust on hanch and beam, the feathers blowing about like fun everywhere. Yet even here there were signs of Christmas, for a withered branch of holly stood in a shapeless vessel on the table. And Adam himself ... There was something even more peculiar than usual about him...

'Why', thundered the Vicar, 'are you wearing three of Mrs Starkadder's red shawls?'

Adam stood his ground.

Flock of sheep, December 1928. (Copyright Garland Collection, West Sussex Record Office)

'I mun have a red courtepy,' he said. 'Iverybody knows that. Ay, the hand o' Fate lies heavy on us all, Christmas and all the year round alike, but I thought I'd bedight meself as Santa Claus, so I did, just to please me little Elfine. And this night, at midnight, I be goin' around fillin' the stockin's, if I'm spared.' ...

The Reverend Hearsay re-seated himself on the table and glanced at his watch. 'Where in Energy's name is everybody? I have to be at the Assembly Rooms to read a paper on The Future of the Father Fixation at eight, and I've got to feed first. If nobody's coming, I'd rather go.'

'Won't ee have a dram o'swede wine first?' A deep voice asked, and a tall woman stepped over the threshold, followed by a little girl of twelve or so with yellow hair and clear, beautiful features. Judith

Starkadder dropped her hat on the floor and leant against the table, staring listlessly at the Vicar.

'No swede wine. I thank you,' snapped the Reverend Hearsay. He glanced keenly round the room in search of the British Port-type, but there was no sign of it. 'I came up to discuss an article with you and yours. An article in Home Anthropology.

'Twere good of ee, Reverend,' she said tiredly.

'It is called Christmas: From Religious Festival to Shopping Orgy. Puts the case for Peace and Good Will very sensibly. Both good for trade. What more can you want?'

'Nothing,' she said, leaning her head on her hand.

'But I see,' the Vicar went on furiously, in a low tone, and glaring at Adam, 'that here, as everywhere else, the usual childish wish-fantasies are in possession. Stars, shepherds, mangers, stockings, fir-trees, puddings ... Energy help you all! I wish you good night, and a prosperous Christmas.'

He stamped out of the kitchen, and slammed the door after him with such violence that he brought a slate down on his back tyre and cut it open, and he had to walk home, arriving there too late for supper before setting out for Godmere...

'Now, missus, have ee got the Year's Luck? Can't make puddens wi'out the Years Luck,' said Adam, shuffling forward.

'It's somewhere here. I forget ---- '

She turned her shabby handbag upside down, and there fell out on the table the following objects:

A small coffin nail
A menthol cone
Three bad sixpences
A doll's cracked looking-glass
A small roll of sticking-plaster

Adam collected these objects and ranged them by the pudding basin. 'Ay, them's all there,' he muttered. 'Him as gets the sticking-plaster'll break a limb; the menthol cone means as you'll be blind wi' headache, the bad coins means as you'll lose all yer money, and him as gets the coffin nail will die afore the New Year. The mirror's seven years' bad luck for someone. Aie! In ye go, curse ye!' And he tossed the objects into the pudding, where they were not easily long distinguishable from the main mass.

'Want a stir, missus? Come, Elfine, my popelot, stir long, stir firm, your meat to earn', and he handed her the butt of an old rifle, once used by Fig Starkadder in the Gordon Riots.

At midnight, when the farmhouse was in darkness save for the faint flame of a nightlight burning steadily beside the bed of Harkaway, who was afraid of bears, a dim shape might have been seen moving stealthily along the corridor from bedroom to bedroom. It wore three shawls pinned over its torn nightshirt and carried over its shoulder a nosebag (the property of Viper, the gelding), distended with parcels. It was Adam bent on putting into the stockings of the Starkadders the presents which he had made or bought with his savings. The presents were chiefly swedes, beetroots, mangel-wurzels and turnips, decorated with coloured ribbons and strips of silver paper from tea packets.

'Ay,' muttered the old man, as he opened the door of the room where Meriam, the hired girl, was sleeping over the Christmas week. 'An apple for each will make 'em retch; a couple o' nutys will warm their wits.'

Everybody was in an even worse temper than usual when the family assembled round the long table in the kitchen for the Christmas dinner about half-past two the next afternoon. One by one they came in, the men from the fields with soil on their boots, the women fresh from hennery and duck filch with eggs in their bosoms that they gave to Mrs Beetle who was just making the custard. Everybody had to work as usual on Christmas Day, and no one had troubled to put on anything handsomer than their usual workaday clouts stained with mud and plough-oil. Only Elfine wore a cherry-red jersey over her dark skirt and had pinned a spray of holly on herself. An aunt, a distant aunt named Mrs Poste, who lived in London, had unexpectedly sent her the pretty jersey. Prue and Letty had stuck sixpenny artificial posies in their hair, but they only looked wild and queer...

At last all were seated and waiting for Ada Doom.

'Come, come, mun we stick here like jennets i' the trave?' demanded Micah at last. 'Amos, Reuben, do ee carve the turkey. If so be as we wait much longer, 'twill be shent, and the sausages too.'

Even as he spoke, heavy footsteps were heard approaching the head of the stairs, and everybody at once rose to their feet and looked towards the door.

The low-ceilinged room was already half in dusk, for it was a cold, still, Christmas Day, without much light in the grey sky, and the only other illumination came from the dull fire, half-buried under a tass of damp kindling.

Adam gave a last touch to the pile of presents, wrapped in hay and tied with bast, which he had put round the foot of the withered thorn-branch that was the traditional Starkadder Christmas tree, hastily rearranged one of the tufts of sheep's wool that decorated its branches, straightened the raven's skeleton that adorned its highest branch in place of a fairy-doll or star, and shuffled into his place just as Mrs Doom reached the foot of the stairs leaning on her daughter Judith's arm. Mrs Doom struck at him with her stick in passing as she went slowly to the head of the table.

'Well, well. What are we waiting for? Are you all mis-hooden?' She demanded impatiently as she seated herself. 'Are you all here? All? Answer me!' banging her stick.

'Ay, Grummer,' rose the low, dreary drone from all sides of the table. 'We be all here.'

Rabbit catcher, 1931. (Copyright Garland Collection, West Sussex Record Office)

PLUM POTTAGE AND PLUM PUDDING

We are all aware that a traditional Christmas dinner finishes with a Christmas pudding. In the late nineteenth century this was more usually termed 'plum pudding' and looked like a cannon ball, having been boiled for hours in the wash-house copper tied in a well-greased and floured cloth, and was served up with a flaming halo of alcohol and a sprig of holly. It is said that Queen Victoria's cooks made 400 plum puddings to be given to the Queen's estate workers during the Christmas period as presents. According to the Queen's maître d'hôtel and chief cook, Charles Elme Francatelli, who wrote A Plain Cookery Book for the Working Classes *in 1861 (London, Bosworth and Harrison, 1861, reprinted in 1993 by Pryor Publications, Whitstable), a simple and affordable version of the plum pudding for the poorest section of the community would include flour, raisins, currants, chopped apples, suet, sugar, eggs, beer (or milk in temperance households), salt and allspice.*

From the journal of a Sussex gentleman, Timothy Burrell, Esq., Barrister-at-law of Ockenden House, Cuckfield, which he kept between the years 1683 to 1714, we learn that in the early eighteenth century the 'cannon ball' form of the Christmas plum pudding had not yet made an appearance – then the tradition was to serve 'plum pottage' (also known as plum porridge or plum broth) – which Burrell had served up to his thirteen guests (apparently a 'mix' of the servant class and 'gentlemen') in between courses no less than three times during the same Christmas feast.

Charles Fleet in his book Glimpses of our Sussex Ancestors *(Lewes, Farncombe & Co., 1882, p. 62) comments on Burrell's entry for 1704:*

One of the most prominent features of Mr Timothy Burrell's Journal – and it marks the benevolence of his character and illustrates the close relations which once existed between the high and lower classes of society, whom he invited to dinc with him at Christmas, and the bills of fare that he provided for them. He commenced this custom in 1691, and he keeps it up to the year before his death (1717). The following is the bill of fare for the Burrell Christmas Dinner of 1706:-

1st January, 1706
Plumm pottage, calves' head and bacon, goose, pig, plumm pottage, roast beef, sirloin, veale, a loin, goose, plumm pottage, boiled beef, a clod (?), two baked puddings, three dishes of minced pies, two capons, two dishes of tarts, two pullets.

It will be remarked that plum pudding, without which no Christmas-day festivities would now be complete, does not figure in Mr Timothy Burrell's bill of fare. Its place is supplied by 'plumm potage' (sometimes called 'plumm broth') which occurs thrice in each bill, and which no doubt stood in the place of, and was the embryo of its more famous

Ockenden House, Cuckfield, home of Timothy Burrell.

ancestor. Minced pies had arrived at maturity; but plum pudding had yet to be invented.

E.V. Lucas in his book Highways and Byways in Sussex *(London, Macmillan & Co. Ltd, 1928, pp. 212-3) supplies an old recipe for the same:*

Plum Porridge, it may interest some to know, was made thus:-
Take of beef-soup made of legs of beef, 12 quarts; if you wish it to be particularly good, add a couple of tongues to be boiled therein. Put fine bread, sliced, soaked, and crumbled; raisins of the sun, currants and pruants two pounds of each; lemons, nutmegs, mace and cloves are to be boiled with it in a muslin bag; and a quart of red wine and let this be followed, after half an hour's boiling, by a pint of sack. Put it into a cool place and it will keep through Christmas.

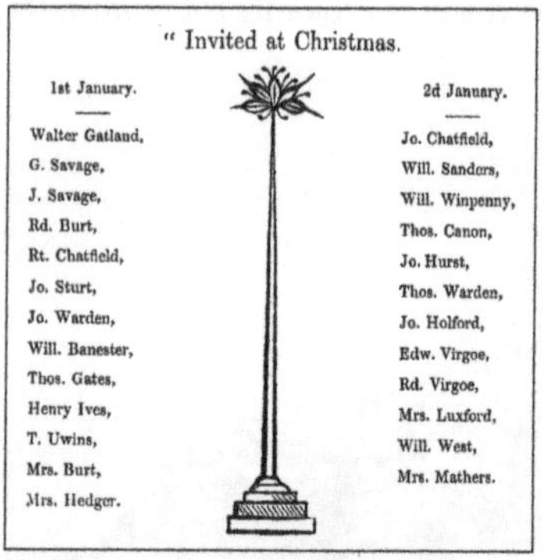

" Invited at Christmas.

1st January.	2d January.
Walter Gatland,	Jo. Chatfield,
G. Savage,	Will. Sanders,
J. Savage,	Will. Winpenny,
Rd. Burt,	Thos. Canon,
Rt. Chatfield,	Jo. Hurst,
Jo. Sturt,	Thos. Warden,
Jo. Warden,	Jo. Holford,
Will. Banester,	Edw. Virgoe,
Thos. Gates,	Rd. Virgoe,
Henry Ives,	Mrs. Luxford,
T. Uwins,	Will. West,
Mrs. Burt,	Mrs. Mathers.
Mrs. Hedger.	

'Invited at Christmas'. The lists of guests from the *Journal and Account-Book of Timothy Burrell Esq. from the year 1683 to 1714.*

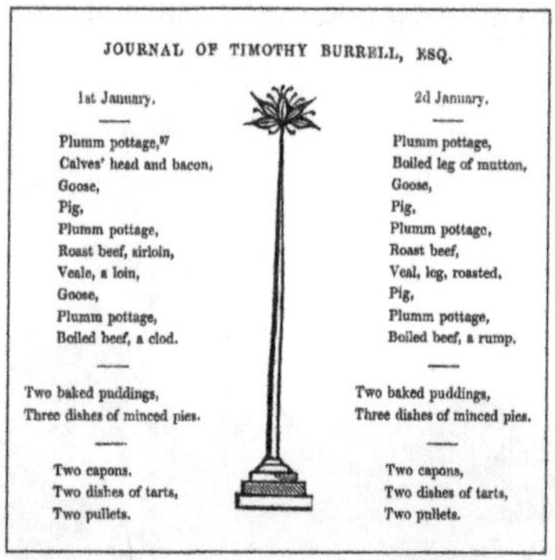

JOURNAL OF TIMOTHY BURRELL, ESQ.

1st January.	2d January.
Plumm pottage,[57]	Plumm pottage,
Calves' head and bacon,	Boiled leg of mutton,
Goose,	Goose,
Pig,	Pig,
Plumm pottage,	Plumm pottage,
Roast beef, sirloin,	Roast beef,
Veale, a loin,	Veal, leg, roasted,
Goose,	Pig,
Plumm pottage,	Plumm pottage,
Boiled beef, a clod.	Boiled beef, a rump.
Two baked puddings,	Two baked puddings,
Three dishes of minced pies.	Three dishes of minced pies.
Two capons,	Two capons,
Two dishes of tarts,	Two dishes of tarts,
Two pullets.	Two pullets.

Christmas dinner menu.

CHRISTMAS IN THE FIRST WORLD WAR WITH THE ROYAL SUSSEX

Cheer up, comrades, we can bide the blast,
And face the gloom until it shall grow lighter;
What though one Christmas should be overcast,
If duty done makes all the others brighter

From Christmas in Wartime *written during the First World War by Sir Arthur Conan Doyle while living at Windlesham, Crowborough*

Sussex men and boys enthusiastically responded to Lord Kitchener's 1914 'The War Needs You!' war recruitment programme. When conscription followed in 1916, the British Army had at its disposal 5 million men but as the war progressed it was realised that this was a war like no other; the war zone was immense and heavy gun bombardment was severely damaging and continuous. Then the scale of casualties on both sides began to beggar belief.

The battalions of the Royal Sussex were obliged to spend their Christmases far from home in a number of theatres of war, not just in Europe but in the Near East and North Africa. The 1st Battalion spent the entire war on the North West Frontier of India; the 2nd remained in France for the duration of the war, living and fighting and spending Christmas in shell-torn wastes of mud and ooze (this battalion alone lost over 1,700 officers and men). Other Royal Sussex battalions served in Gallipoli (Turkey), Egypt and Palestine before being sent to France. Back home in Sussex, the women, now being drawn of necessity into the workforce, could do little except write comfort letters and knit socks and blankets to be sent to the troops.

This is an account of Christmas spent by the Royal Sussex in Jerusalem, 1917, from the Sussex County Magazine:

Christmas 1917 was memorable for the torrential rains which beat relentlessly upon the Royal Sussex which had been holding the outpost lines engaged in isolating and 'pinching out' the Turks in Jerusalem, where General Allenby, desirous of achieving his object without fighting in or shelling of Jerusalem itself, had secured its surrender on 9th December. The beds of all the wadis were roaring torrents, drowning camels, harassing transport and wearying the men. On Christmas Day such torrents fell that bivouac sheets were useless against it. Thousands of small rivulets poured off every rock, defying drainage and soaking everyone. The battalion cooks could not even manage hot tea, and the Royal Sussex Christmas dinner consisted of bully beef, wet biscuit and cold water! Shortage of rations, especially in view of appetites sharpened by keen mountain air, made it doubtful whether the position could be maintained. But Boxing Day witnessed another success. There was increased liveliness among the enemy Turks, who on that day launched a counter-attack to recapture Jerusalem. But our Intelligence had made known the Turks' zero hour, with the result that their efforts proved a costly failure.

By the end of the war the Royal Sussex had lost 6,800 men. Their names are recorded in the Regimental Chapel of St George, Chichester Cathedral.

'Your Country Needs You'. The poster which called recruits to the Colours in 1914 and 1915.

TWELFTH NIGHT

By Hilaire Belloc

Hilaire Belloc (1870–1953), poet and author, was born into a very comfortable professional Parisian household but the year was one of political unrest, when the Paris Commune was erecting barriers around the city and civil war, as well as war with Prussia, seemed imminent. While he was still a tiny baby, the family fled to England (they claimed to have taken 'the last train' out of Paris). On their return they found the family home totally devastated – wrecked and looted by Prussian soldiers. With their fortune even further reduced they moved to Slinden in Sussex and this county for Belloc (though he never lost his sense of being Anglo-French) became 'home'. English public school followed, French military service, British citizenship, an Oxford degree, a career as a writer and then marriage to an Irish-American girl who was also a fervent Catholic. In 1906 Belloc moved his growing family to King's Land, a 'shandyish' house in the village of Shipley, near Horsham, part of which dates back to the fourteenth century, and with which he will be forever identified.

The following Christmas poem is typical in its celebration of the almost surreal beauty of the South Downs under a dark winter's sky, and tells us of Belloc's restrained religious impulse to join the joyous 'company of travellers' – more mundanely Catholics possibly en route to Midnight Mass:

As I was lifting over Down,
A winter's night to Petworth Town,

I came upon a company
Of Travellers who would talk with me.

The riding moon was small and bright,
They cast no shadows in her light:
There was no man for miles a-near.
I would not walk with them for fear.

A star by Gumber glowed,
An ox across the darkness lowed,
Whereat a burning light there stood
Right in the heart of Gumber Wood.

Across the rime their marching rang,
And in a little while they sang;
They sang a song I used to know,
Gloria In Excelsis Domino.

The frozen way those people trod
It led towards the Mother of God;
Perhaps if I had travelled with them
I might have come to Bethlehem.

Shipley Mill, 2004.

THE AVALANCHE ON THE SOUTH DOWNS

From the Sussex Weekly Advertiser, *January 1837*

On Christmas Eve in 1836 and following a severe snowstorm, an avalanche fell from the edge of the Downs and overwhelmed a row of seven cottages that stood under the Downs in South Street, Lewes. Fifteen people were buried in snow and rubble and of these eight were brought out dead. The victims were William Geer (82), Joseph Wood (16), Mary Taylor (42), Phoebe Barden (45), Maria Bridgeman (31), Mary Bridgman (11), Jane Books (25) and Susan Haywood (30).

Their bodies were laid before the poor house and a committee heard the evidence. A child witness had seen a crack open in the snow 'which continued to grow wider until a large quantity came down with extreme violence and on reaching the houses threw them down immediately'. One survivor, James Rook, a labourer, had spoken to Mary Taylor and begged her minutes beforehand not to go into her cottage but she 'popped in to get a shawl' and 'was caught in the street'. Robert Hyam, landlord of the Schooner, whose beer shop faced the line of houses that were destroyed, had warned several inhabitants the night before that a fall was imminent and only four minutes before the fall ran 'down the passage' telling the cottagers to leave everything and get out and save themselves. He was actually talking to Mrs Barden and Mrs Bridgman when they were overwhelmed by the snow, and tried to help them but had to move back to save his own life. The verdict was accidental death. The dead were buried at South Malling and their names recorded on a tablet within the church.

This poem was published in the Sussex Weekly Advertiser *in January 1837, just a week or so after the event, and records the grief felt by the community:*

The snow-storm came on a Christmas night,
And it pil'd its flakes on a cliff's broad height;
And there it lay in its fleecy pride,
When the cold sun gleam'd on the mountain's side.

And the cottagers, dwelling beneath the hill,
Reckless of danger, regardless of ill,
Busied themselves in domestic care –
Mother and daughter and child were there.

The old man close to the fire-side stood,
To quicken the course of his torpid blood;
And the budding infant, with its glances sweet,
Gambol'd and crew at that old man's feet.

At length came a sudden rushing sound,
And the avalanche made its fatal bound;
It dealt destruction to all beneath,
And whelm'd the inmates in darkness and death.

Sad and loud was the funeral wail
That was borne abroad on the biting gale;
They gather'd the victims no pow'r could save,
And buried them all in one common grave.

The snow is melted, the storm is past,
And hush'd is the voice of the wintry blast;

Lightly and mild will the summer breeze blow,
And the Dead be forgotten who slept in the snow.

A 'gentleman' who had witnessed the fall gave the Sussex Weekly Advertiser *his eyewitness account:*

[It was] a scene of the most awful grandeur. The mass appeared to him to strike the houses first at the base, heaving them upwards and then breaking over them like a gigantic wave to dash them bodily into the road; and when the mist of snow, which then enveloped the spot, cleared off, not a vestige of a habitation was to be seen – there was nothing but an enormous mount of pure white.

The scene which ensued was heart-rending. Children were screaming for their parents and women were rushing through the streets with frantic gestures in search of their off-springs while in the midst of all the consternation, men were hastening from all quarters for the purpose of extricating the sufferers.

A description of the severe winter conditions which preceded the snowfall were reported in the Sussex Weekly Advertiser *(also reprinted in the* Sussex County Magazine *of 1927):*

Scarcely has the excitement caused by the effect of the late tremendous hurricane subsided, when it becomes our duty to record another, and in its results, a still more calamitous visitation. On the morning of Saturday se'n night, a heavy quantity of the snow which fell was not unprecedented: but unfortunately a strong gale of wind sprang up, which, sweeping the ground in places nearly bare, in others accumulated the snow into drifts of incredible depths, so that all traces of roads and tracks were lost, and any communications between the different towns in this part of the country was entirely prevented by huge barriers of solid snow, which had been by the force of the wind, heaped in masses in some places to the depths of 20 feet, wherever the inequalities of the ground offered a lodgement for it. The oldest inhabitants declare that they never remember such a deep snow. So effectively were the roads choked up on Monday that the town of Lewes was blockaded from the slightest communication with the surrounding country, except by means of the river.

Not a vehicle was seen in the streets during the whole day, most part of the shops were shut, and all trade was at a standstill. The Brighton mail cart arrived here and returned on Sunday evening with the greatest difficulty; and it was only by the utmost exertion and perseverance that Mr. Leney's coach, which started from Lewes the same evening, could be dragged to Brighton, having been three hours on the road; on its arrival the coachman, Ford, was in such a state of exhaustion that he was obliged to be lifted from the box. It was found to be totally impossible to forward the London mail from Lewes that night, and the next morning Mr. Saxby, the postmaster with a laudable [word obliterated] to prevent any public inconvenience from the stoppage of the mail, despatched a messenger with the bags and chaise and four who proceeded as far as Malling Hill, on the outskirts of the town, where the road was completely blocked up with a barrier of snow several feet in height, and he was compelled to relinquish the task. It was only on Wednesday morning at eleven, that the mail (which was due on Tuesday morning at five) arrived, having been brought by men on foot from East Grinstead.

On Monday night a large party of labourers were set to work on the Lewes and Brighton road, but they were not able to complete a sufficient passage for vehicles until Thursday, when the coaches again commenced running with four horses each. A communication was also opened in Maresfield, but the drifts were laid so thickly over the road above that place, that Mr. Sincock, who arrived with his coach on Saturday afternoon from London, was compelled to remain until the following Friday, where he started with six horses.

The almost entire suspension of every kind of commerce in the town of Lewes, was doubtless attended with extreme inconvenience; but this informed only a minor source of regret, when compared with the awful loss of life occasioned by the snow in that town.

It was observed on Monday that the violence of the gale on the previous night had deposited a continuous ridge of snow, from ten to fifteen feet in thickness, along the brow of that abrupt and almost perpendicular height, which is based by South Street and the Eastbourne road, where tons upon tons seemed to hang in a delicately turned wreath as lightsome as a feather, but which, in fact, bowed down by its own weight, threatened destruction to everything beneath.

The Revd Edward Boys Ellman, retired vicar of Berwick, set down his memories of the event in old age and thought there were eight houses destroyed by the avalanche:

The following winter [1837] there was another snowstorm, but though not generally so deep as that of 1836, [it] overhung Cliffe Hill [Lewes] in wreaths, and falling down in an avalanche it crushed eight houses, burying sixteen people of whom eight were dead when they were dug out. On the spot now stands the Snowdrop Inn, so named because the snow there dropped.

William Thompson's Personal Account of the Lewes Avalanche, *written around 1870, describes the poignant ruin of Christmas food and decorations which, whilst heightening the horror of the circumstance, gives us a glimpse of the seasonal festivities of ordinary people in Lewes at this period, showing that even slightly before the advent of the influence of Victoria and Albert, small houses had their own individual decorations and Christmas fare:*

The furniture and clothes of the poor sufferers were mixed in utter confusion with broken roofs, black bricks from chimneys and ruined crockery while occasional pieces of cake and plum pudding, intermingled with holly and evergreens, exhibited bitter memorials of the festivities of Christmas.

Gideon Mantell, Lewes doctor and archaeologist, recorded in his diary for Christmas Day that year:

Christmas Day – a snow storm began last night and has continued through the day and everything is most gloomy and wretched. I returned to my den this evening wet through from walking in snow up to my knees – the fire out – the smoke coming down instead of up.

The Lewes avalanche, 1836.

CHRISTMAS IN THE LEWES CHILDREN'S HOMES, 1933

Traditionally, children's care homes were run with severe discipline, and though special 'treats' and a Christmas dinner were always provided, the essence of a real 'family Christmas' could not be recreated in an institution, despite the kindness of individuals who freely gave up their time to join in the homes' celebration of the day:

A very happy day was spent at the Lewes Children's Homes, Avenue House, in the gaily decorated wards. The dining room was decorated with laburnum and the schoolroom with clematis, by the Misses Jarrott, Brunson and Mawford, assisted by some of the older girls.

Dinner included turkey and plum pudding and was served about mid-day. Councillor C. Newling, Dr. and Mrs R.S. Tooth. Mr. and Mrs. Newling, Jun., Miss H. Nevill and the Rev. C.S. Ensell (chaplain assisting the Matron Mrs. M. Ladbrook) and staff. The children had previously been the recipients of handsome Christmas stockings (the gifts of Mrs. E.K. Lee) and various other toys sent by residents of Lewes and district.

In the evening, Mr. and Mrs. Gibbons of the Avenue, visited the Houses, where Mr. Gibbons impersonated Santa Claus, distributed balloons, and sweets and chocolates.

Christmas turkeys on a Sussex farm in the early 1930s. (Copyright Garland Collection, West Sussex Record Office)

A HOME COMING

From The Book of Sussex Verse, *first printed in 1914*

Sussex man A.T. Bell (1875-1918), having suffered an injury in childhood that left him severely handicapped, was unable to fight in the First World War. This poem may reflect Bell's sincere hope and belief (shared by most people in 1914) that the young Sussex men who had marched so bravely off to war that year would all be home in their native Sussex for Christmas, and that the war would have ended. Bell, an Oxford graduate and academic of some distinction, lived in Storrington:

Sussex windmill in winter. (Copyright Garland Collection, West Sussex Record Office)

Sussex brooding o'er dreams of winter
Mists o'er valley and down and plain,
Winds flecked red from the burning woodland,
Hillsides grey in a drift of rain,
Land of my heart, friend, bride, and mother,
Dreaming Sussex, we meet again.

Thakeham pines, with a surge like thunder,
Swaying aloft o'er fern grown brown;
Homesteads, lost in a waste of water
Where sunset reddens on Pulborough town;
Racing cloud -crack and house-rooks whirling
Over the beeches on Duncton Down.

Wide white roads of the south-land calling
Feet that have trodden the ways of pain,
Village, glowing a firelit welcome
To hands that have beaten men's doors in vain.
Motherland calling, children yearning
Dreaming Sussex, we meet again.

MEMORIES OF A PETWORTH CHRISTMAS DINNER, 1812

From Tales of Old Petworth
by John Osborn Greenfeield

This mouth-watering and informative account of a copious Christmas dinner eaten in 1812 when he was only ten years old came from the pen of John Osborn Greenfield (1802-69), who in later life became the landlord of the Angel Inn, Petworth. John Osborn Greenfield was raised by his beloved 'grandmamma' in Petworth but only set down these recollections after his retirement, in the 1860s, entitling his memories Tales of Old Petworth. *They tell us how a Georgian Christmas was celebrated amongst the middle classes; here there is no Christmas tree, no Christmas cards, no Christmas crackers and no Christmas carols sung. Christmas Day was celebrated in a very special and low-key way – a visit to church and a good Christmas dinner. Eating, drinking, card games and song are essentially the order of the day and the goodwill embraces the servant class:*

The party consisted of Mr and Mrs Sherwin, of Moor, Mr and Mrs Elliot of Gunter's Bridge, Mr John Wild, of Ripley, a retired officer of high rank in the excise, a fine, noble-looking old man, the very picture of an old beau of the time...

At a quarter before two the hostess, with a face of a deep scarlet, here entered the parlour to say that dinner was ready, and requested the ladies to follow her. They did so without a second bidding, and the gentlemen in a body went after them, and the host brought up the

Town crier in the snow, Petworth. (Copyright Garland Collection, West Sussex Record Office)

rear, but I was led in by the hand of my grandmamma, and took a seat by her side. The dining room was the front kitchen, the usual sitting room of the family ... And in it was a grate large enough for roasting and their general cooking ... At the fire there was yet roasting three fine ribs of beef, and in a dish placed under it to catch the last rich droppings lay a huge mass of French beans; they had been preserved in salt from the growth of the previous summer, and Mrs Garland prided herself on their nice green colour, notwithstanding the long time (as she told us), that they took in boiling. In the pan lay also sundry slices of pudding, saturating the hot dripping.

The Soup

When we were all seated the hostess asked if everybody would take soup, and there being no dissenting voice she got up, and with the assistance of her one servant girl, Betty Weeden, and her son George, the basins were filled from the pot over the fire and set before each of us. In them we found some small pieces of meat, onions, turnip, carrot &c. &c. But oh!, this soup! How disappointed I was. It was merely a poor, thin, watery kind of broth, and lots of great round spots of yellow grease floating on the surface.

The Meat
But by this time George and the maid had beef, pudding, and beans on the table, and from some back cooking place were bought in a couple of fine roasted fowls, a large ham, a dish of potatoes, and a blue and white basin containing about a quart of rich melted butter, with chopped parsley in it.

Plum Pudding
The dinner was completed by two huge puddings: swimming in blazing rum.

Bread and Cheese
Celery and bread and cheese finished the feast. There was ale, but no wine at dinner, but each of the men drank off a glass of gin after the cheese, and the ladies sipped a little carraway water, and as it was nice and rich and sweet I was indulged with a spoonful out of grandmamma's glass.

The servants
There was a round (table) in the corner (of the room) at which were seated two of Mr Garland's journeymen, Jack Baxter and Bob Munday, and the maid also. The servants were served by the hostess from our table, and they partook of everything like the guests. Indeed they joined in the conversation, for they had lived many years with their good natured, kind old master.

Dessert and Wine

When the cloth was removed, apples of various sorts, nuts, walnuts, and almonds and raisins were put on the table, with three or four sorts of home-made wine, and gin and rum to qualify their acidity ... Foreign wines were never at that time seen on a tradesman's table; they were too expensive, and Hollands had long been out of use. When the ladies had returned to the parlour, pipes and tobacco were introduced.

Songs and Stories

After a pipe and grog ... Jack Baxter volunteered a song or two, which he sang in a first-rate manner ... Songs, toasts, and funny stories, some not suited to modern society, went round the table. My good old granddad, old dadda as we always called him, had a beautiful voice, and sung song after song, each better than the preceding, and all went on gloriously until about half-past four.

Tea

Then (in came) the hostess, to prepare the tea. She was followed by the maid, bearing in one hand a half-gallon loaf, and in the other a huge mass of yellow salt butter to make the toast ... (and) her master, by permission of his wife, ordered her to sing 'Barbara Allen', which, assisted as before by her young master, she did very nicely and sweetly.

The Gentlemen join the Ladies

Soon after five, the gentlemen joined the ladies at the tea-table, when chat and gossip went on ding-dong. There were no pianos, or musical young ladies and gentlemen, nor photographic albums in 1812 in Petworth.

Whist

When tea was over, my grandmamma, with Mr John Wild for her partner, played at whist against Mrs Servais and her husband, for silver three-pennies, and the other ladies made a party at drawboard with beans for counters, at a penny per dozen. The gentlemen not card players, after a quiet nap by the fire, went back to the room in which we had dined, to resume their grog and pipes till the time came to lay the cloth for supper.

Supper

At ten o'clock supper was ready. It consisted of the remains of dinner, and when it was over, soup and grog and pipes and tobacco, for the ladies made no objection to the smoke, went on for another hour, and then we started with clogs and pattens, candles and lanthorns, to plod our way home through the snow, ankle deep.

Petworth in the snow.

SUSSEX CHRISTMAS ALE

The Shoreham 'Bushellers', from the Sussex Daily News, 5 January 1883

The Red Lion pub near the old wooden bridge over the Adur at Old Shoreham dates back to the sixteenth century. In the winter of 1792 a highwayman called James Rock was arrested there after boasting in the bar of a highway robbery he had participated in at Hove. As Tennyson recounts in his gruesome poem 'Rizpah', after his execution his mother collected his bones and buried them at St Nicholas church, a stone's throw

Interior of the Red Lion Inn, Old Shoreham.

from the pub. Tamplins, the famous Brighton Brewers, owned the house in Victorian times, when the following custom was described:

A new corn measure was filled with ale, and served 'free' to all comers at the Red Lion Inn at Shoreham on Christmas Day. This custom appears to have been carried on for over 80 years, and the new corn measure was decorated with flowers and green paper it was said to resemble a large cauliflower' The corn measure was filled twice, and the ale was ladled out with a pint-size mug and then drunk from glasses. Those who drank this free beer were known as the 'Bushellers'.

The famous Harvey's Brewery at Lewes also does a distinctive and very strong Christmas ale (alcohol 8.1 per cent) with a picture of Father Christmas on its label – 'a strong, heavily hopped seasonal drink with an original gravity of 1086-1090'. Until Christmas 2004, this was only served in half pints at the John Harvey Brewery tap, and having sampled a pint-and-a-half one lunchtime this year, one of the authors can understand why! Harvey's have been brewing at the Bridge Wharf Brewery, on the banks of the River Ouse, since the late eighteenth century.

Harvey's Brewery, 2004. (Photograph Geoff Doel)

GREAT FROSTS IN SUSSEX

The severe winter conditions of 1846/47 and 1881 are here recalled by the Revd Edward Boys Ellman in his Recollections of a Sussex Parson:

In the winter of 1846/47 there was another heavy fall. I was staying at Clapham with my sister at the time, and walked through the snow to Berwick, intending there to take the train to Lewes, where I had a meeting. On arriving at Berwick Station, finding that the railroad was blocked, I waded through the snow to Lewes, and then on to Landport. There was no mark in the snow of anyone or any vehicle having preceded me until I reached Lewes.

In 1881 the railroad was again blocked. A train was snowed up near Polegate, and a lady passed the night in a signal-box, as she could not even get to the station.

The first two winters of the Second World War were immensely severe with below-zero temperatures, sharp frosts and deep snowdrifts that made some roads impassable. An article in the 1940 Christmas edition of the Sussex County Magazine, Vol. 3, suggests that those who had been born in the late Victorian period would be reminded of similar weather conditions they had endured in their youth:

Youngsters of King Edward's reign – though even they may be now middle-aged – have sniffed at stories of those older who babble of the winters of their youth. Now that we may discuss the iron frost and snowdrifts of January and early February the wheel comes full circle and the snowstorms of 18 January 1881 and the ice-blocked Thames at

London Bridge of 1895 come up for comparison. They show that from Christmas 1939 to mid-February 1940 we have had a winter only of the real old sort – weeks of iron-bound earth and continuous skating, roads blocked by snowdrifts many feet high. At last veterans alive can complacently assure today's youth that what it regards as unprecedented in severity is only a gauge of long successions of winters when persons still living were at school.

Details of just how severely Sussex was affected in the winter of 1939 come in this account by PC Spink from the Sussex County Magazine:

The immense aggregate of degrees of frost resulted in the very rare spectacle of the sea frozen on the South Coast. Off Thanet and the North Kent Coast the ice extended some distance out to sea, and many shallow waters off the Sussex coast were fringed or covered with ice, especially in shallow creeks and harbours such as Bosham, Chichester, Emsworth, Langstone, and skating was reported on the shallows of Haslar creek off Gosport. Comparatively thick ice was reported off the Witterings which piled up into long ridges parallel with the shore.

The amount of precipitation for January was low until the 27th and 28th, when over an inch of rain fell, and half a foot of snow fell on the 29th and 30th, the snowfall being far heavier in West Sussex.

One of the most remarkable features of an extraordinary month was the night of the 27th and the 28th. This was caused by rain falling from an extensive strata of air warmer than that immediately above the frozen earth, consequently freezing upon reaching the ground and resulting in all solid objects being coated with ice varying from half an inch to an inch in thickness.

Trees, hedges, gates, stubble, buildings – everything was glazed. Bents of grass appeared as glass rods, telephone wires were each estimated to carry 80-90lb weight of ice between adjacent posts. The

Rooks building their nests.

resulting damage can be imagined, for wires were down in places for mile after mile, and hundreds of poles were either uprooted or snapped off.

Many curious results of this glazed rain ... have come to light. Birds were seen frozen by their feet to branches of trees where they had roosted on the previous night. They vainly fluttered their wings in their efforts to fly away and had to wait until the sun or a change of wind finally thawed the ice. A resident of Maresfield reported having to release his fantail pigeons from the roof of his house to which they had frozen. Rooks were reported to have fallen from trees with their wings frozen together, and live sheep were seen frozen by their wool to gorse bushes on the Downs...

A sad feature of the frost was the damage caused to trees. Curiously enough, deciduous trees, notably beeches and oaks, suffered most, and conifers least. Many woods, especially in West Sussex, towards the Hants border, looked as though they had been under gun fire, with broken boughs lying everywhere. The weight of ice had caused occasional trees to snap off half way up.

Early in February a thaw set in with heavy rain, but this change was short lived; the frost returned on the 10th ... However, it did not last, and a sharp snowstorm from the SE, on the night of the 16th produced six inches. The wind backed to the NE during the day and then followed a remarkably sudden and intense frost on the morning of the 18th when a surface sub-zero temperature of -1.5 recorded frost – the lowest recorded at Slinfold this winter ... It must have been caused by an intense cold-wave in the early hours of the morning, for by dawn the wind had veered to the SE again, and the temperature was rapidly rising. This freak frost virtually concluded the winter proper – a winter without parallel.

CHRISTMAS IN BRIGHTON HOSPITAL DURING THE SECOND WORLD WAR

By June Longly

As Christmas 1940 approached, Germany was in possession of the whole European coastline, and those who lived on the Sussex south coast lived in daily expectation of a German invasion by sea and attacks by air. The Sussex people had already lost access to their beaches which had been rolled with barbed-wire entanglements; in Brighton they had also seen their two piers partially blown up and small artillery guns set along the top road of the seafront, with a big gun positioned in Black Rock Gardens, Lewes Crescent. All over the county signposts were taken down to confound the enemy (and often succeeded in confounding the local population). Austerity became the order of the day as ration books were issued for the duration of the war with meat, sugar, butter and eggs always in short supply. Fearing mustard-gas chemical attacks, the government issued gas masks to adults and provided red 'Mickey Mouse' masks for babies and young children. Identity cards were issued and people learned to memorize their National Registration number.

The advice now given was to 'stand ready' while the male population was either called up on compulsory military service or taken into the Home Guard. Each household was given a government booklet, The Protection of your Home Against Air Raids, which counselled families to seek shelter in a cellar, if there was one, and to 'be prepared' with tins of food (and a tin opener!), drinking water, candles, matches, chamber pots, toilet paper, disinfectant, first-aid equipment, reading matter, children's toys, bedding and a wireless. Anderson shelters came later and were constructed in gardens and school playgrounds, while Harrison shelters were erected inside the house; windows were taped-up against bomb blasts and a compulsory 'blackout' was rigorously enforced.

Six months before Christmas 1940 the Germans had begun the series of bombing attacks now known as the Battle of Britain and just three months before mass air-raid attacks on British cities started, which continued until the end of the war. Sussex towns and cities were not the target, but the county inevitably suffered continuously as German fighter planes returning from raids, or on a reconnaissance mission, dropped whatever bombs they had left over the English coast before making for home. The civilian population gradually got used to planes being spotted overhead at night and searchlights raking the skies until sirens wailed the all-clear.

The following is an account of Christmas spent in the Royal Sussex County Hospital, Brighton, by Mrs June Longly (née Miles), a survivor of the bomb that fell on the Odeon cinema, Brighton, in September 1940. A German bomber had been chased by a Spitfire and dropped its load – six bombs in all – over six locations in Brighton, including Edward Street, Hereford Street, Upper Rock Gardens, Bedford Street, and Paston Place, site of the cinema in Kemp Town. Fifty-two people were killed:

My enduring memory of a Christmas in wartime is due to the fact that I spent it in hospital. It was Christmas 1940 and I was one of the casualties in the bombing of the Odeon cinema, Kemp Town, along with my mother and brother Philip. On Saturday 14 September 1940, a German bomber returning from a raid dropped six bombs over Sussex before crossing the Channel. One was a direct hit on the Odeon cinema at Paston Place, opposite the old brewery. It was about four o'clock in the afternoon or a little after and we were enjoying a matinee performance of *The Ghost Goes West*. I've been told that there were nearly three hundred people in the cinema. Almost all were children and their mothers. The bomb made a direct hit and the roof caved in. They probably used ambulances to convey some of the survivors to the nearby hospital, that I don't remember, but they took me away in a double-decker bus which they commandeered (in fact they commandeered all kinds of vehicles).

We were all taken to the Royal Sussex County Hospital, Eastern Road. I was to stay there for seven months. This was a hospital for adults – there was no children's ward – and at first I was put in a bed next to my mother who lost her leg. My mother told me that I didn't talk for three weeks. My father came to see us as soon as he found out where we were and was distraught not only by our state but by the fact that he could not find my brother Philip. Dad wandered all over the hospital, probably thinking the worst, and was guided to a ward by the sound of a child sobbing. It was Philip. He had lost a finger in the blast and had a severely damaged hand as well as having shrapnel in his leg. In the general chaos of admitting the wounded he had been registered as Mills instead of Miles which is why my father could not trace him at first.

But Christmas day 1940 was made as enjoyable as possible for us by the efforts of the doctors and nurses. The ward was decorated with paper chains and at lunchtime we were entertained by the staff. Amid much laughter and comic antics they pretended to carve the turkey – the 'turkey' was a doctor lying on a large table. The doctor doing the carving had a huge knife and fork and he produced endless strings of giant sausages much to the enjoyment of the patients. I hasten to add that we all enjoyed a traditional Christmas dinner after all the entertainment – turkey with all the trimmings and a delicious Christmas pudding. One of the Sisters gave me a Christmas present – a beautiful little brooch in the shape of a basket of flowers. I kept it for a very long time only to lose it many years later on a visit to a cinema!

EDDI'S SERVICE

By Rudyard Kipling

Rudyard Kipling was sent by his Anglo-Indian parents to be educated in private boarding schools in England. A lonely and sensitive child, his schooldays were hugely cheered when his beloved Aunt Gorgy (Lady Burne-Jones), his mother's sister, invited him to spend December with her children. From that time on Christmas became for Kipling 'a paradise'. Aunt Gorgy's records of the children's Christmas activities in the 1870s are typical of the age (see Georgiana Burne-Jones' Memorials of Edward Burne-Jones, Vol. II, 1904, pp. 45-6). Firstly came the 'magic lantern', with a presenter who talked through boxed sets of slides, the child audience sitting excitedly and expectantly in the dark. Then followed the game of 'snap-dragon' in which raisins, steeped in alcohol in a huge Victorian meat-plate, were placed in the centre of a table and the alcohol set alight. As the raisins ignited they flew into the air – and the fun began as everyone attempted to catch the raisins using their mouth only. On Christmas Eve Lady Burne-Jones, fully aware that the children would be too excited to retire early to bed, encouraged her grown-up guests (many of them famous artists and writers) to tell the children fairy tales and ghost stories.

As a married man and a father, Kipling elected to live in Sussex and spent several Christmases, first at Rottingdean (a house which is now the public library) and then in the beautiful seventeenth-century property, Batemans, on the outskirts of Burwash. Many of his collections of children's stories and poems use legendary Sussex material, such as Rewards and Fairies (1910) which features the story 'The conversion of St Wilfred'. This story deals with the seventh-century conversion of Sussex to

Christianity, details of which are given in Bede's Ecclesiastical History of the English People and Eddius's Life of Wilfrid. Kipling prefixes the following Christmas poem to his story, which features Eddius ('Eddi') as priest at Manhood End (Church Norton), a site originally connected to Wilfrid's bishopric at Selsey. The Sussex King Aethilwalh granted Wilfrid 9,000 acres of surrounding land:

Eddi, priest of St Wilfrid
In the chapel at Manhood End,
Ordered a midnight service
For such as cared to attend.

But the Saxons were keeping Christmas
And the night was stormy as well,
Nobody came to service
Though Eddi rang the bell.

'Wicked weather for walking'
Said Eddi of Manhood End,
'But I must go on with the service
For such as care to attend.'

The altar candles were lighted, -
An old marsh donkey came,
Bold as a guest invited
And stared at the guttering flame.

The storm beat on at the windows
The water splashed on the floor,
And a wet yoke-weary bullock
Pushed in through the open door.

'How do I know what is greatest,
How do I know what is least?
That is My Father's business,'
Said Eddi, Wilfrid's priest.

'But three are gathered together -
Listen to me and attend,
I bring good news, my brethren!'
Said Eddi, of Manhood End.

And he told the Ox of a manger
And a stall in Bethlehem,
And he spoke to the Ass of a Rider
That rode to Jerusalem.

They steamed and dripped in the chancel
They listened and never stirred,
While, just as though they were Bishops
Eddi preached them The Word.

Till the gale blew off on the marshes
And the windows showed the day,
And the Ox and the Ass together
Wheeled and clattered away.

And when the Saxons mocked him
Said Eddi of Manhood End,
'I dare not shut His chapel
On such as care to attend.'

Church Norton, 1989. (Photograph Geoff Doel)

THE MOTE IN THE MIDDLE DISTANCE

By Max Beerbohm

Rye in winter has to be one of the prettiest towns in Sussex, when its hilly cobbled streets and wealth of medieval and Georgian buildings are snowcapped and frosted over. One of its most attractive and important Georgian buildings is Lamb House, built in the eighteenth century and erstwhile home to James Lamb, vintner, Collector of Customs for Rye and Shoreham, and thirteen times mayor of the town. In the winter of 1726, which was a severe one with gales and heavy snowfalls, the Lamb family's life was marked by two exciting events. As Lamb's wife fell into labour, news was brought to the house that the ship carrying King George I from Hanover had been driven off course and was washed ashore on nearby Camber Sands. One can imagine the consternation in the Lamb household and indeed the town as they realised that they would have to play host to royal guests. Mayor Lamb rode off to Camber in a snowstorm with his municipal officers and brought the King back to his own house. George was given the best bed (probably only recently vacated by Mrs Lamb who had been delivered of a boy child – she had been removed upstairs to an inferior room). Needless to say the new baby was named George in the king's honour and the sovereign graciously consented to be the child's godfather.

Many years later, in 1900, Henry James, the American novelist, acquired the freehold of Lamb House for £2,000. Here 'the Master' played host to many of the established writers of the day including G.K. Chesterton, Joseph Conrad, Ford Madox Ford, Rudyard Kipling and H.G. Wells. It was here he wrote his three most lauded novels, The

Ambassadors, The Wings of the Dove and The Golden Bowl. Max Beerbohm (1872-1956), essayist, cartoonist and wit, was a frequent visitor to Lamb House. In his collection of essays, A Christmas Garland (1912), Beerbohm humorously parodies the styles of several of his contemporaries. This is Beerbohm's witty Christmas tale written in the style of Henry James in which he irreverently exaggerates 'the Master's' dense, convoluted style, and deep moral interest in English tradition. The moral dilemma here is gloriously trite – two Victorian children, Keith and Eva Tantalus, having woken early on Christmas morning, consider whether they should unpack their Christmas stockings or wait for their nurse to appear before they do so:

It was with the sense of a, for him, very memorable something that he peered now into the immediate future, and tried, not without compunction, to take that period up where he had, prospectively left it. But just where the deuce *had* he left it? The consciousness of dubiety was, for our friend, not, this morning, quite yet clean-cut enough to outline the figures on what she had called his 'horizon', between which and himself the twilight was indeed of a quality somewhat intimidating. He had run up, in the course of time, against a good number of 'teasers': and the function of teasing them back-of, as it were, giving them, every now and then, 'for what'- was in him so much a habit that he would have been at a loss had there been, on the face of it, nothing to lose. Oh, he always had offered rewards had ever so liberally pasted the windows of his soul with staring appeals, minute description, promises that knew no bounds. But the actual recovery of the article – the business of drawing and crossing the cheque, blotched though this were with tears of joy – had blankly appeared to him rather in the light of a sacrilege, casting, he sometimes felt, a palpable chill on the fervour of the next quest. It was just this fervour that was threatened as, raising himself on his elbow, he stared at the foot of his bed. That

Lamb House, Rye, 2004.

his eyes refused to rest there for more than the fraction of an instant, may be taken – *was*, even then, taken by Keith Tantalus – as a hint of his recollection that after all the phenomenon wasn't to be singular. Thus the exact repetition, at the foot of Eva's bed, of the shape of the pendulous at the foot of *his* was hardly enough to account for the fixity with which he envisaged it, and for which he was to find, some years later, a motive in the (as it turned out) hardly generous fear that Eva had already made the great investigation 'on her own'. Her very regular breathing presently reassured him that, if she *had* peeped into 'her' stocking, she must have done so in sleep. Whether he should wake her now, or wait for their nurse to wake them both in due course, was a problem presently solved by a new development. It was plain that his sister was now watching him between her eyelashes. He had half expected that. She really was – he had often told her that she really was – magnificent; and her magnificence was never more obvious than in the pause that elapsed before she all of a sudden remarked, 'They so very indubitably *are*, you know!'

It occurred to him as befitting Eva's remoteness, which was a part of Eva's magnificence, that her voice emerged somewhat muffled by the bed-clothes. She was ever, indeed, the most telephonic of her sex. In talking to Eva, you always had, as it were, your lips to the receiver. If you didn't try to meet her fine eyes, it was that you simply couldn't hope to: there were too many dark, too many buzzing and bewildering and all frankly not negotiable leagues in between. Snatches of tother voices seemed often to intrude themselves in the parley; and your loyal effort not to overhear these was complicated by your fear of missing what Eva might be twittering. 'Oh, you certainly haven't, my dear, the trick of propinquity!' Was a thrust she had once parried by saying that, in that case, *he* hadn't – to which his unspoken rejoinder that she had caught her tone from the peevish young women in the Central seemed to him (if not perhaps in the last, certainly in the last but one, analysis) to lack finality. With Eva, he had found, it was always safest to 'ring off'. It was with a certain sense of his rashness in the matter, therefore, that he now, with an air of feverishly 'holding the line', said, 'Oh, as to that!'

Had *she*, he presently asked himself, 'rung off'? It was characteristic of our friend – was indeed 'him all over' – that his fear of what she was going to say was as nothing to his fear of what she might be going to leave unsaid. He had, in his converse with her, been never so conscious as now of the intervening leagues; they had never so insistently beaten the drum of his ear; and he caught himself in the act of awfully computing, with a certain statistical passion, the distance between Rome and Boston. He has never been able to decide which of these points he was psychically the nearer to at the moment when Eva, replying, 'Well, one does, anyhow, leave a margin for the pretext, you know!' Made him, for the first time in his life, wonder whether she were not more magnificent that even he had ever given her credit for being. Perhaps it was to test this theory, or perhaps merely to gain time, that he now raised himself to his knees, and leaning with outstretched arm towards the foot of his bed, made as though to touch the stocking which Santa Claus had, over-night, left dangling there. His posture, as he stared obliquely at Eva, with a sort of beaming defiance, recalled to him something seen in an 'illustration'. This reminiscence, however – if such it was, save in the scarred, the poor dear old woebegone and so very beguilingly *not* refractive mirror of the moment – took a peculiar twist from Eva's behaviour. She had, with startling suddenness, sat bolt upright, and looked to him as if she were overhearing some tragedy at the other end of the wire, where, in the nature of things, she was unable to arrest it. The gaze she fixed on her extravagant kinsman was of a kind to make him wonder how he contrived to remain, as he beautifully did, rigid. His prop was possibly the reflection that flashed on him that, if *she* abounded in attenuations, well, hang it all, so did *he*! It was simply a difference of plane. Readjust the 'values', as painters say, and there you were! He was to feel that he was only too crudely 'there' when, leaning further forward, he laid a chubby forefinger on the stocking, causing that receptacle to rock ponderously to and fro. This effect was more expected than the tears which started to Eva's eyes and the intensity with which 'Don't you,' she exclaimed, 'see?'

'The mote in the middle distance?' He asked. 'Did you ever, my dear, know me to see anything else? I tell you it blocks out everything. It's a cathedral, it's a herd of elephants, it's the whole habitable globe. Oh, it's, believe me, an obsessiveness!' But his sense of the one thing it *didn't* block out from his purview enabled him to launch at Eva, a speculation as to just how far Santa Claus had, for the particular occasion, gone. The gauge, for both of them, of this seasonable distance seemed almost blatantly suspended in the silhouettes of the two stockings. Over and above the basis of (presumably) sweetmeats in the toes and heels, certain extrusions stood for a very plenary fulfillment of desire. And since Eva *had* set her heart on a doll of ample proportions and practicable eyelids – *had* asked that most admirable of her sex, their mother, for it with not less directness than he himself had put into his demand for a sword and helmet – her coyness now struck Keith as lying near to, at indeed a hardly measurable distance from, the border line of his patience. If she didn't *want* the doll, why the deuce had she made such a point of getting it? He was perhaps on the verge of putting this question to her, when, waving her hand to include both stockings, she said, 'Of course, my dear, you *do* see. There they are, and you know I know you know we wouldn't, either of us, dip a finger into them.' With a vibrancy of tone that seemed to bring her voice quite close to him, 'One doesn't,' she added, 'violate the shrine – pick the pearl from the shell!'

Even had the answering question 'Doesn't one just?', which for an instant hovered on the tip of his tongue, been uttered, it could not have obscured for Keith the change which her magnificence had wrought in him. Something, perhaps, of the bigotry of the convert was already discernible in the way that, averting his eyes, he said, 'One doesn't even peer.' As to whether, in the years that have elapsed since he said this, either of our friends (now adult) has, in fact, 'peered', is a question which, whenever I call at the house, I am tempted to put to one or other of them. But any regret I may feel in my invariable failure to 'come up to scratch' of yielding to this temptation is balanced, for me, by my impression – my sometimes all but throned and anointed certainty – that the answer if vouchsafed, would be in the negative.

A WARTIME RECIPE FOR ALMOND SHORTBREAD

From the 19 January edition of the
Sussex and County Herald, *1940*

The wartime rationing of sugar and meat was introduced on 8 January 1940. Householders were ordered to register in advance 'with a retailer of their choice' and issued with rationing books. Newspapers and magazines soon began to produce 'wartime' recipes for housewives which took into account the limited food resources available. This recipe, which is suitable for a New Year's party, is lauded for the small amount of sugar used:

> ALMOND SHORTBREAD
> Here is a recipe for almond shortbread which only takes one ounce of sugar and is very easy to make:-
> 6 ounces flour
> 1½ ounces ground almonds
> 4 ounces margarine
> A good pinch of salt
> 1 ounce sugar
>
> Rub the fat into the flour, sugar, salt and almonds, and knead all thoroughly. Press into a sandwich tin and bake in a moderate oven until slightly browned.

THE SUSSEX WASSAIL

From John Broadwood's Old English Songs from the Weald of Surrey and Sussex

The term 'wassail' is made up of two Anglo-Saxon words meaning 'be healthy'. Geoffrey of Monmouth, writing in 1136, tells the story that it was first used in Britain by Renwein (Rowena in later versions), the daughter of the Saxon mercenary leader Hengist, to greet the British King Vortigern, who fell in love with her and married her.

The tradition of wassailing was a midwinter visitation ritual to bring good fortune for the ensuing year and consisted of a procession of wassailers carrying a wassail bowl from door to door and singing songs which asked for food, drink and money, and wished good luck to the household. Many elaborate wassail bowls survive from the Middle Ages and the custom continued well into the eighteenth century and has not completely died out. But in the late eighteenth and nineteenth century, wassailing was gradually replaced by carol singers singing religious carols, though sometimes with the odd wassail song in their repertoire. A tradition of wassailing survived at the Elephant and Castle pub at West Chiltington at Christmastime until the First World War, and was photographed in 1910.

The wassail songs were not religious, but sometimes their tunes were taken over and reused for carols. This happened in the case of God Rest Ye Merry Gentleman, *the tune of which is in the ancient Dorian mode (i.e. key of D using the white notes only on a piano). By chance the earlier wassail song survives as it was collected John Broadwood, Sussex vicar*

Wassailing at the Elephant and Castle, West Chiltington, 1910.

and uncle of the famous Sussex folksong collector Lucy Broadwood, when it was sung on his doorstep by some boy mummers.

John Broadwood collected this song in the 1820s; he later privately published it in his Old English Songs from the Weald of Surrey and Sussex *in 1843. John Broadwood described his collection of songs as 'sung by the Peasantry' of the Surrey and Sussex Weald and as 'collected by one who has learnt them by hearing them sung every Christmas from early childhood by the country people who go about the Neighbouring Houses singing, 'wassailing' as it is called at that season.' His purpose was 'to rescue them from oblivion and to afford a specimen of genuine Old English Melody.'*

The words of the song firmly locate it as a wassail rather than a religious carol. Christ and Mary are not mentioned, but the song is concerned with food and drink and the annual cycle of sympathetic magic effecting good luck. As well as the door-to-door wassailing tradition, the song also invokes wassailing bees and apple trees, both of which traditionally occurred in Sussex. The vicar of Amberley, the Revd G. Clarkson, collected the words of a song thought to have been sung to the bees on Twelfth Night from an old man in his parish:

> Bees, oh bees of paradise, does the work of Jesus Christ.
> Does the work which no man can.
> God made bees and bees made honey.
> God made man and man made money.
> God made great men to plough and to sow.
> God made little boys to tend the rooks and crows.
> God made women to brew and to bake.
> And God made little girls to eat up all the cake.
> Then blow the horn!

Essentially, though, the words of The Sussex Wassail *convey the cold and damp condition of the wassailers as they trudge from house to house and wait on the doorsteps in the hope of the food and drink and money which seal the good luck compact between householders and seasonal wassailers:*

> A wassail, a wassail, a wassail we begin,
> With sugar plums and cinnamon and other spices in,
>
> Chorus: With a wassail, a wassail, a jolly wassail,
> And may joy come to you and to our wassail.
>
> Good master and good mistress as you sit round the fire,
> Remember us poor wassailers who travel through the mire.
> Good master and good mistress, if you should be but willing,
> Come send us out your eldest son with sixpence or a shilling.

If there's any maids within this house as I suppose there's none,
They'd not let us stand a wassailing so long on this cold stone.

We've wassailed all this day long and nothing could we find,
But an owl in an ivy tree and her we left behind.

We'll cut a toast all round the loaf and set it by the fire;
We'll wassail bees and apple trees until your hearts desire.

Our shoes are very dirty, our shoes are very thin,
They lack a little silver to line them well within.

Hang out your silver tankard upon your golden spear,
We'll come no more a-wassailing until another year.

APPLE WASSAILING – THE 'DUNCTON HOWLERS'

Apple wassailing, or howling as it was termed in Sussex because of the din, is a piece of sympathetic magic which used to be prevalent in cider apple districts of England in which a libation of cider punch was given each year to a representative cider apple tree to invoke a bountiful crop of cider apples. In the west of England male orchard workers tended to wassail their own trees, often firing guns, either to arouse the tree or frighten away evil spirits. But in Sussex semi-professional groups of boys, known as 'howling boys', moved from orchard to orchard in specific locations between Christmas Eve and Twelfth Night to wassail trees for money, food and drink. Sussex has the first recorded specific reference in the country (not counting a general allusion in a poem by Robert Herrick) when Giles Moore, rector of Horsted Keynes, recorded in his diary for 26 December 1670: 'Gave to the howling boys 6d'.

Charlotte Latham mentions the custom in her book Some West Sussex Traditions Lingering *in 1868:*

It is the custom in the cider districts of Sussex to 'worsle' the apple trees on New Year's Eve, and for several succeeding days, and it is considered unlucky to omit doing so. Farmers give a few pence to the worslers, who form a circle round the trees and sing at the top of their voices:

> Stand fast root,
> Bear well top,
> Pray God send us,
> A good howling crop,

Every twig,
Apples big,
Every bough,
Apples enow,
Hats full, caps full,
Full quarter sacks full,
Holloa, boys, holla! Huzza!

And then all shout in chorus, with the exception of one boy who blows a loud blast on a cow's horn. Last New Year's Eve the mother of a sick boy told me that her poor child was sadly put out because he was not able to 'worsle' his grandfather's apple trees; and it is quite certain that both mother and child expected a total failure of the apple-crop in the grandfather's orchard to follow the omission.

The most famous and long-standing apple-howlers in West Sussex were the Knight family of Duncton, who 'worsled' the Duncton environs every Twelfth Night until around 1923. The only known photograph of traditional apple howling in the south-east dates from around 1897 and shows the leader Richard 'Spratty' Knight – the Duncton miller – his wife and his son Arthur (who led the team in its decline for a few years after the First World War). In the photograph the miller is wearing a brightly patterned costume with a string of apples around his neck and a large decorated straw hat with apples round it; he is blowing a copper and brass hunting horn, which appeared in an exhibition in 1982 and was inscribed 'Thomas Bridger, Duncton Beagles, November 1860'. Mrs Knight is holding a jug of cider and a Twelfth Night cake.

The following are two descriptions of apple-howlers. The first is a letter in the West Sussex Gazette, *5 January 1967, from Mr E.F. Turner of Westhampnett, the 'youngest of the family living at Mill Farm, Duncton' during the last days of the wassailing there:*

The first Captain of the Wassailers I remember was Dick Knight, who had a dark spade beard. We children would become very excited as 'Old Christmas Eve' (January 5th) got nearer, and on the night we used to be continually opening the back door to listen for the wassailers.

At last we would hear them, faintly at first and gradually getting louder. It sounded as though they split into two parties, one coming down the lane on one side of the millpond and the second through the orchard on the other. What we heard was something like this:

> ALL TOGETHER: 'Here stands a good old apple tree.' (Or 'Nanny tree', or 'Green Pippen tree', etc.)
> FIRST PARTY: 'Stand fast root.'
> SECOND PARTY: 'Bear well top.'
> FIRST PARTY: 'Every little bough.'
> SECOND PARTY: 'Bear apples enow'.
> FIRST PARTY: 'Every little twig'.
> SECOND PARTY: 'Bear apples big.'
> FIRST PARTY: 'Hat fulls.'
> SECOND PARTY: 'Cap fulls.'
> FIRST PARTY: 'Three score sack fulls.'
> CAPTAIN: 'Holler, boys, holler.'

Then there would be a burst of horn-blowing, shouting and a general racket. Sometimes a big bad word would float across when someone trod in a hole or tripped over a root.

When they reached the house, they would come into the big kitchen, with its pump, sink, bread-oven, three coppers and fireplace to sing songs and drink cider. One would be carrying the enormous cow horn, and the Captain would have on a robe made of something like a flowered cretonne and a straw hat with big apples all round the wide brim, and a bow of wide ribbon.

His song was about 'Three bold fishermen rolling down the tide' and someone with 'three golden chains hanging dangling three times round'. The tune was marvellous ... I think his son sang 'Two Little Girls in Blue'.

Fred Lock from Upwaltham was a regular. He sang 'Bid Adieu to Old England'. You might get anything from John Rowe or Bernard Connor. People said they could remember enough songs to last for two hours or so. We generally had 'The Farmer's Boy', 'If I Were a Blackbird', 'Seagull', and 'Farmer Giles' among others.

My sisters used to stand near the doorway leading out of the kitchen, ready to go to the cellar for more cider or else to vanish for the time being if a song seemed to be getting salty.

When they left, we used to go outside to hear more wassailing, the voices getting fainter and fainter as they went through another part of the orchard on their way to the next stopping place.

In the course of time Dick Knight's place as Captain was taken by his son ... Arthur. I think the wassailers stopped coming in the early twenties, but in 1920 or thereabouts I heard Jack Court sing 'The Sunshine of Your Smile' and someone else, who seemed put out because he did not know any old songs, sang 'Back Home in Tennessee'.

The Sussex Daily News *account for 8 January 1919 shows the custom struggling for survival, with Arthur Knight having moved out of Duncton:*

The war has done its best to kill our customs and habits, but customs die hard. And so one finds that the quaint ceremony of 'wassailing' or charming the apple trees observed at the Down village of Duncton is one which has so far survived. Nevertheless things are not as they used to be. In years gone by when the old chief, Mr Dick Knight, was alive 'wassailing' night was always a great event in the village. When the old chief died his son, Mr Arthur Knight, promised he would carry on the tradition of the village, and he has faithfully fulfilled his promise. Every year he re-visits his native village on old Christmas Eve to head the wassailers in their pilgrimage to the orchards. This year his followers numbered only three. The smallness of the band was not surprising for, as the chief remarked, 'there is no-one about now' – many 'wassailers' are engaged in sterner work than the charming of apple trees. Despite the small number of 'wassailers' and the downpour of rain, the usual visits were made to Mrs Court's, Lavington Park, Mr Seldon's, Mrs Knight's, at the home of the old chief, and the mill 'neath the apple trees.

The song sung by Richard Knight is a very well-known folksong in Sussex and it is impossible to know which version Richard Knight sang to accompany the apple howling custom at Duncton. We have chosen a version collected by the Sussex and Hampshire collector Clive Carey, from

The Duncton Howlers, c. 1897.

Leonard Glaysher in the village of Borden in East Hampshire in 1911. This is not far from Duncton and is therefore contemporaneous with Richard Knight's apple wassailing. Many early carols were not originally written for the Christmas/New Year season, but later became attached to it. The fisherman in this carol is clearly an allegory of Christ, the fisher of men gathering souls, and the motif of Christ as bridegroom is one relevant, for example, to the condition of nuns, who regarded Christ as their husband. But The Bold Fisherman *song has elements of a May seduction song in which it was presumably the lady who was originally laid down, rather than 'fishing gown'! There is thus an interesting conflation of sacred and secular, of celibacy and fertility:*

As I walked out one May morning
Down by the river side,
And there I beheld a bold fisherman

(Chorus)
Come rowing down the tide.
Come rowing by the tide
And there I beheld a bold fisherman,
Come rowing down the tide.

'Good morning to you, bold fisherman
How came you a-fishing here?'
'I've come a-fishing for your sweet sake
All down this river clear.'

He rowed his boat up to the shore
And unto him this lady went,
And in taking hold of her lily-white hand
Which was his full intent.

Then he pulled off his fishing gown
And laid it on the ground,
And there she beheld three chains of gold
Came wrinkling three times round.

Then on her bended knees she fell
And as for mercy called,
'I call-ed you a bold fisherman
But I think you are some lord.'

'Rise up, rise up, my dear' cried he
'From off those bended knees,
There's not one word you've said or done
That has least offended me.'

Then come unto my father's house
And married we will be,
And you shall have a bold fisherman
To row you on the sea.

Brighton fishermen landing a catch of mackerel, c. 1900.

WHEN CHRISTMAS WAS CANCELLED AND WITCHES WERE ABROAD

During the Commonwealth and Protectorate (1649-60) the Lord Protector, Oliver Cromwell, was persuaded (it is said against his better instincts) to dissolve the Long Parliament following allegations that its members were 'drunkards', 'corrupt', 'unjust' and 'living in open contempt of God's commandments' – even though it had fought the Civil War and beheaded Charles I. The new Members of Parliament were Puritans – farmers, gentlemen, lawyers, scholars – some fundamentalists and fanatics and some not – carefully selected from Puritan congregations up and down the country. The Puritans had long objected to the usage and ceremonies in the Church of England which had derived from the Roman Catholic Church – processions, instrumental church music, religious images, and above all the great liturgical feasts of the year, especially Christmas.

Seizing their chance, the new Parliament passed a law which removed Christmas from the calendar – thus the whole seasonal festival was cancelled. It was now forbidden to go to church on that day, to take time off work, to feast and make merry, even to eat Christmas mince pies. 25 December therefore became a normal working day and the Twelve Days of Christmas with their Lord of Misrule and Twelfth Night cake were no more.

There is a certain irony in the fact that despite the Puritans' acknowledged disbelief of all things 'mystical' they actively helped intensify the popular belief of the day that there were those in the community who had supernatural powers by encouraging people to report cases of witchcraft to the authorities. During the so-called 'witch hysteria' of the seventeenth century, perhaps a score of Sussex women and men (the records are incomplete) were identified by members of the public and reported to Puritan bodies as witches. The accusations were always taken seriously – those charged were imprisoned and examined and if the charges were 'proved' witches were put to death by hanging. Most 'witches' were old, poor, and probably senile; brutal questioning and maltreatment at the hands of the authorities ensured that confessions were obtained confirming every worst fear – that they consorted with the Devil and had supernatural powers which enabled them to pass through locked doors, fly through the air, shape-shift, as well as destroy life, limb and livestock using demonic agency. Included in the Puritan list of witches were the 'cunning folk' – the herbalists, conjurors and healers who often employed charms or prayers in their 'cures'; for the Puritans their 'craft' embodied unacceptable practices and beliefs inherited from the Old Faith.

The following indictment was brought against a Sussex woman, Widow Jane Shoutbridge of Withiam. The year was 1652 and Shoutbridge was accused of 'overseeing' a twelve-year-old girl named Mary Muddle during what would once have been termed the Christmas season. To 'oversee' is to 'look malevolently' with the implication that some evil power works on the victim. This was the second charge in two years brought against so-called witches in Withiam by Mary Muddle's family, who sought to attribute their anorexic or perhaps consumptive daughter's 'wasting' to witchcraft. A distinguishing feature of the indictment is the prosecutor's misogynist violence of language – there is unbridled contempt in the way in which he addresses the woman standing before him, despite the fact Shoutbridge may be dirty and stinking having been retained in custody for six months.

Sussex fortunately did not suffer from the itinerant self-styled 'Witchfinders' who were patrolling Britain at this period and claimed unerring discovery of witches in the community – at £2 and £3 per head. It comes as a relief to know that good sense prevailed and Widow Shoutbridge was discharged:

The jurors for the Lord Protector of the Commonwealth of England, Scotland and Ireland, upon their oaths, doe present that Jane Shoutbridge, late of Withiam in the county of Sussex aforesaid, widow, the 30th day of Dec in the yeare of our Lorde one thousand six hundred fifty twoe, being a common witch and enchantress, not having God before her eyes, but being moved or seduced by the instigation of the Divell, the said 30th day of Dec of the yeare aforesaide with force and arms etc. Att Withiam aforesaid, certain wicked and Divelish arts called witchcraft, enchauntments, charms and sorceyres in and uppon one, Mary Muddle, spinster of the age of 12 yeares, wickedly, divelishly, feloniously, wilfully and of her malice before thought did use, practyse and exercise on the said Mary Muddle then and there feloniously and of the malice before thought did bewitch and enchaunt by reason of which said wicked and divelish Arts called witchcrafts, enchauntments, Charmes and Sorceyres by her the said Jane Shoutbridge in and upon the said Mary Muddle, used, practysed and exercised on the aforesaid Mary Muddle the said 30th day of Dec in the year aforesaide and divers other dayes and times as well before as afterwards at Withiam aforesaide in the County aforesaide in her body was greatly wasted, consumed, pyned and harmed against the public peace and against the form of the Statute in this case made and provided.

A seventeenth-century woodcut.

EPIPHANY AND A TiME OF GIVING

Ever since the Three Wise Men brought gifts to the stable the Christmas season has been marked as a time of giving from the rich to the poor. Here are two accounts of Sussex nobility in the nineteenth century distributing largesse and seasonal goodwill in communities that were much more tight-knit and feudal than today:

The Annual Fawn Supper, Frant
By Andre Page. From Sussex Life, *Vol. VII, 1971*

A wonderful and traditional Christmas supper was held at Frant for over 80 years prior to the war, and this was known as 'The Annual Fawn Supper'. A fawn from the Eridge Park Estate was given for the feast by the Marquess of Abargavenny, and all the employees on his Sussex estate were guests on that evening. The roasted fawn – plus all the trimmings – was washed down with good Sussex ale brewed by the famous – but now extinct – firm of Ware's of Frant and after the Loyal Toast, 'baccy was smoked from long-stemmed 'Churchwarden' pipes.

New Year's Day at Maresfield Park
From Hone's Every-Day Book, *1828*

A practice which well deserves to be known and imitated is established at Maresfield Park, Sussex, the seat of Sir John Shelley, Bart., MP. Rewards are annually given on New Year's Day to such of the industrious poor in the neighbourhood as have not received parish relief, and have most distinguished themselves by their good behaviour and industry, the neatness of their cottages and gardens, and their constant attendance at church, etc. The distribution is made by Lady Shelley, assisted by other ladies; and it is gratifying to observe the happy effects upon the character and disposition of the poor people with which this benevolent practice has been attended during the few years it has been established. Though the highest reward does not exceed two guineas, yet it has excited a wonderful spirit of emulation, and many a strenuous effort to avoid receiving money from the parish. Immediately as the rewards are given all the children belonging to the Sunday school and national school lately established in the parish are set down to a plentiful dinner in the servants' hall; and after dinner they also receive prizes for their good conduct as teachers, and their diligence as scholars.

Day labourer in black Sussex frock, outside Bignor church, 1880.

TUCKS CHRISTMAS CARDS, 1940s-STYLE

Advertisement from the Sussex Express and County Herald, *1940*

Is it because the thought of no Christmas at all with loss of the glad spirits and precious memories awakens a determination to observe Christmas, if not as usual, with all its accustomed joys at least with as much heartiness as possible that the sight of the old familiar Christmas cards with their treasured sentiments and traditional pictures banishes any doubt that personal greetings and kind remembrances must not be allowed to perish on earth?

Any question whether Christmas shall be forgotten this year is dismissed by a glance at all the many beautiful cards of topical design and infinite variety which Raphael Tuck & Son have put at the service of the public to enable them to keep their Christmas merry still. The greater the anxiety, the more the need of cheer and cheer in abundance will be circulated by the cards of a thousand different designs which Tucks have made available for the coming season. As one would expect, the services have been specially remembered. There is a special card for every branch of our Forces and cards which express the sentiments of all towards the gallant lads who are standing between us and tyranny. The RAF is honoured by sky blue creations symbolising the much that so many owe to so few while the Navy and Army have not been forgotten.

Then there are the old Christmas wishes expressed in many beautiful and artistic forms besides the humorous subjects with an appeal to the young and messages of remembrance and patriotism to cement ties of brotherhood which unite the Empire.

Tucks productions are this year better than ever before. And if this is true of the cards, it also applies to the beautiful calendars for 1941 which will be in greater demand than ever as useful Christmas presents.

THE PELHAM DOLE

From The Diary of Thomas Turner

The Georgian shopkeeeper, churchwarden and diarist Thomas Turner describes many fascinating customs from the East Hoathley area, including the traditional money and food distribution to the poor on St Thomas's Day:

We arose at three to perform our task, viz: some of the ancestors of the Pelham family have ordered that, on this day (for ever) there should be given to every poor man or woman that shall come to demand it, 4d; and every child, 2d; and also to each a draught of beer, and a very good piece of bread. I believe there was between seven and eight hundred people relieved of all ages and sexes, and near £9 distributed, besides a sack of wheat made into good bread, and near a hogshead and half of very good beer.

CHRISTMAS TERM AT LANCING COLLEGE

By Sam Brooke, 1860

Lancing College is amongst a number of fine new public schools in Britain which were created in the early part of the nineteenth century. It had its origins in an earlier school, the Saints Mary and Nicolas School at Shoreham, which was relocated to Lancing in 1857/58. The following fascinating account is from the diary of Victorian schoolboy and Lancing scholar, Sam Brooke, and is his entry for the month of December 1860. Although this is the lead-up to Christmas, here there is no mention of a Christmas tree, decorations, carol singing or the sending of Christmas cards. Sam, a prefect and high-minded and serious young man of sixteen, is totally focused on his end of term examinations. Had he been able to look into the future he would have been relieved to find that he would soon become Captain of the School and then later take a Master's Degree at Corpus Christi, Oxford. Sam was one of eighteen children; his father was a solicitor and the family lived at Margate:

December
1-Saturday
In the morning our examinations began. Did a piece of Latin prose without Dictionaries or Grammars. Found it tolerably easy; better than I expected. In the afternoon a match was played with Brighton College: they got one goal and so beat. Watched the game with Skinner for a short time. Saw Mr. Mertens in the course of the afternoon. In the evening did nothing particular; composed, however, a piece called 'Uriola', or the 'weeping maid of Greece.'...

Lancing College chapel.

2-Sunday

At Chapel at 11 Mr. Wilson preached. In the afternoon went out for a short walk, but spent most of the time in copying out 'Uriola' in the Poetry Book, and reading over again pieces of 'Eric', by F.W. Farrar. In the evening commenced a new piece, not entitled at present by any name. It is upon the drowning of three boys on the 3rd of June, 1858. The style of it is à la 'Lady of Shallot' by Tennyson...

3-Monday

In the morning the examination was continued. We did a piece of Greek prose. In the afternoon had a Thucydides paper, which on the whole was not very hard. In the evening continued the new piece without a name and finished it by 9 p.m.

Latest Intelligence 7.30 p.m.! At 7 p.m. this evening the last quarter's marks, together with the result of both quarters. It would be needless to recount the former; the latter was Jackson, Brooke, Hilton, Slocock, Johnson....

4-Tuesday

In the morning had Cicero for examination to translate. The pieces were on the whole favourable. The afternoon would have been half a holiday had it been fine, but since that was not the case continued our examination doing Elegiacs and Hexameters. Felt very tired indeed towards the close of this afternoon...

5-Wednesday

In the morning our examination was continued. We had a Homer paper, which was on the whole easy. At twelve went out solus round by Lancing and the cricket field. Saw the new draining system operation going on ... In the afternoon did Greek Iambics from the fourth Georgic; rather a curious proceeding, certainly. In the evening did not have chapel till 8 p.m. when Dr. Lowe preached from Rev. Vii. 2-3 – a very good sermon indeed, it being the eve of St. Nicolas Day.

Latest Intelligence R. Deane was this day at 12 birched for having dirty trousers, a rather mild thing to be birched for!...

6-Thursday (St. Nicolas Day)

In the morning till about 11 read different tales of History out of a book from Mr. Wilson's Library. After that time went out (solus) to Lancing or thereabouts as on the preceding day. At Dinner had better grub than usual, and dessert afterwards, with the usual toast of 'Floreat Collegium'. Afterwards did nothing particular, but got late for chapel, thinking it was in the evening at 7. In the evening went up to Mrs. Wilson's and played on the piano there.

7-Friday

The whole of this day was devoted to the Mathematical examination, of which there were 4 papers:-

i. Euclid Paper from 9 – 10 a.m.
ii. Arithmetic Paper from 11 – 12 a.m.
iii. Mixed Paper from 3 – 4 p.m.
iv. Algebra Paper from 4 – 5 p.m.

8-Saturday

In the morning had an examination in Greek and English History; the paper was a very good one indeed, and I answered all the questions. At 12 made some attempt at learning my Virgil Repetition and partially succeeded. In the afternoon stayed in and wrote. It was wet...

Untoward Event. At 10.45 this evening a most unfortunate event happened. I was saying my prayers, and considerable irreverence was displayed by the Lower Dormitory. On getting up I was further insulted and, getting into an uncontrollable rage, I went and reported them to Mr. Wilson bodily. Mr. Wilson then came into the dormitory, inquired about it, blamed Slocock the other prefect, threatened the rest, and left. I got into bed, but could not get out of hearing all kinds of promiscuous and uncomplimentary sentiments circulating round. It was unfortunate, certainly, that I did what I did, and will be very unpleasant hereafter.

9-Sunday

At 11 o'clock chapel Mr. Wilson preached. In the afternoon did nothing in particular. In the evening wrote and played upstairs in the drawing-room to Mrs. Wilson.

Late Dormitory Affair. This morning the general antipathy was at its height against me on account of last night's business, but at

1 o'clock I made friends with the bulk of the malcontents, and the matter thus passed over. On the whole this apparent evil has turned out considerably beneficial, for up to the latest hour this evening my former enemies were assiduously civil and polite.

Wrote another note to Revd. F.M.D. Mertons, requesting a loan of £1 10s for journey money.

10-Monday

In the morning the examinations were continued in the forms of Greek Testament. The paper I found very fair on the whole. In the afternoon went on with Roman History, and Blunt's History of the Reformation. In evening tried to learn some Repetition and partially succeeded.

Repetition. This half we take up 560 lines of Virgil and 420 lines of Homer, in all 980 lines. The Homer is peculiarly difficult and I cannot but apprehend a downfall...

11-Tuesday

In the morning had a rather easy Virgil paper. We take up the 1st and 4th Georgics, of which I knew preciously little about the former. However, the pieces were easy and I flattered myself on my good fortune. Had my hair cut at 12. In the afternoon played my last game at Football this half.

12-Wednesday

In the morning took place the Extra Work Examination. Personally, I was examined in Juvenal. In the afternoon followed the Repetition. I went in at 4; said the Virgil and broke down in the Homer. In the evening went down to the Provost's to tea. All the boys about to leave, and those whose fathers the Provost knew, went also. Spent a very pleasant evening...

13-Thursday

In the morning, a little after 9 a.m. the Vth Form went into the Head Master's Library. He told us that with regard to those who had broken down in Repetition he should say no more. He said that the result of the Examination was barely satisfactory, but that he would not blame us as we had done so well in the half. In our form Jackson was the only fellow who got a prize. He afterwards had us each in separately. In the afternoon went down to Shoreham to change a Post Office order, etc. In the evening, played, talked, etc. etc.

Serious Row took place in the evening about some furniture in the Under School-room being damaged. The whole school threatened to be kept back unless the culprits were discovered. On this, Jones and Burt confessed to the deed. They were kept back, poor fellows...

Lancing College and chapel.

14-Friday

Started from the College at 6. From Shoreham at 7.30. From Brighton at 8: reached Reigate at 9 a.m. Had breakfast there, made up accounts and started for Margate at 1.10, arriving there at 4 p.m. Did a little Virgil in the evening!

Accounts, December 1860

		£	s	d
1.	Lent to Follett	1		
4.	Spent for Stamp	1		
8.	Lent to C.A. Watts			2
13.	To Blaker for Red Cap	1	9	
	To Badcock for Toothbrush			7
	To Drummond and Boot-boy	2	3	
14.	Bridge & Passage to Reigate	5	6	½
	For Breakfast at Laker's, Reigate	2	6	
	Grub and Station, Book, &c &c	2	8	
	Passage from Reigate to Margate	10	0	
15.	To Mrs. Jarmand	3	6	
	Velocipede & Grub at Sawyer's	1	0	
17.	Subscription to New Church School feast	2	6	
21.	For mendage of my Watch at Fagg's	6	6	
22.	To a poor woman	1	0	
24.	To Mr. Clarke, ye blower	6		
28.	For a thermometer at Bentley's	1	3	
	For an apple at Epp's	1		
29.	For Stamps	4		
	Gave in Church as Offertory	1	0	

THE MURDERERS' TABLE

On Christmas Day 1170 the Primate of all England, Thomas à Becket, celebrated Mass before the people of Canterbury, after which he delivered a fiery sermon in which he excommunicated a number of King Henry II's friends and supporters. This news was hurried to the King in France who allegedly declared 'Will no one rid me of this meddlesome priest?' Interpreting this as a command, four Norman knights, Richard le Breton, William de Tracy, Hugh de Moreville and Reginald Fitzurse crossed the Channel on 28 December in wintry seas and rode to the Archbishop's palace at Canterbury in Kent. They arrived in a storm and in the dark on 29 December. Hearing servants cry 'Armed men in the cloister' and the shouts of the knights, 'Reaus! Royal knights, king's men, king's men', Becket's monks hurried the Archbishop into the sanctuary of the cathedral but the Normans followed and cut Becket down with their swords, piercing his body and slicing his head, after which they returned to Sussex to one of the knights' manor house at Old Malling. Although this house is not open to the public, the stone table on which the murderers laid their swords can be seen in Anne of Cleve's House, Lewes. The following extract, which deals with Lewes in the medieval period, is from J.M. Connell's The Religious History of Lewes *written in 1931. It indicates how the murder of Becket created one of the greatest centres of pilgrimage in Europe and how the table itself became the centre of a Sussex medieval legend. Becket's Feast Day (29 December) became a popular day in which to make a pilgrimage to Canterbury as the gloriously decorated shrine was revealed to pilgrims and special dispensations given:*

On days of public rejoicing there would be a grand procession through the town, in which the Prior and his monks, coming by way of Rotten Row (*route du roi?*) would join the parochial clergy and choirs, the guilds of handicrafts, mounted knights clad in glittering steel, archers and men-at-arms, – with banners flying and trumpets blowing and all the other accompaniments of mediaeval pageantry. The proceedings of such days would include a miracle-play or a morality-play, performed in a church or church-yard; and despite ecclesiastical disapproval, oft repeated, there would probably be a tournament in the Castle Yard, as exciting for the spectators as a race meeting or a football match is now.

A town that was so frequently thronged with visitors, and which, through the Priory and the Friary, was kept in constant touch with the Continent, could not fail to be affected by the religious and social movements of the time. Among these was the crusading movement. In 1253 St. Richard, Bishop of Chichester, preached a crusade along the south coast and Lewes would be included in his itinerary. At the altar of the Church of the Holy Sepulchre many a crusader must have

The stone table from Old Malling in Anne of Cleve's House. (Photograph Geoff Doel)

made his vows and prayers before embarking on his perilous enterprise. In our High Street were often seen groups of pilgrims on their way to the shrine of St. Thomas à Becket – pilgrims of the various types described with such inimitable humour and vivacity in Chaucer's *Canterbury Tales*. These pilgrims would make their devotions at the Church of St Thomas in the Cliffe. On their way out of the town they would halt at Old Malling, and listen with bated breath while their guide told them how, on the second night after the murder of Becket, his assassins were resting in his Manor House there, and how their weapons and saddles, which had been laid on a table in the room where they sat, were thrown on the floor, and on being replaced, were thrown again, as if by an unseen hand and in abhorrence of their wicked deed.

MIDHURST MAIL ROBBERY

From The Wonderful Weald *by Arthur Becket*

On the 5th of December 1797 the post boy, carrying the mail from Petworth to Haslemere, was stopped about two miles from Midhurst at a place called North Heath, between seven and eight o'clock at night, by two men dressed in white round-frocks. One of them seized the horse and threatened to blow out the brains of the post boy if he was not quick in unstrapping the mail. Thereupon the robbers took the bags of letters sent from Arundel, Petworth and Midhurst, destined for London, and so made off.

The Postmaster-General having offered a reward of two hundred pounds, over and above the sum of forty pounds granted by Act of Parliament for each person to those who gave information which would lead to the apprehension of highwaymen, the Drewets were in due time arrested for the affair ... The two men, of whom Robert was the elder and William the younger were born in Midhurst, of poor but honest parents.

...At the gallows William, who left a widow and six small children, declared his innocence, 'and hop'd that the spectators would take a warning and not hang people wrongfully'. After the execution the bodies of the brothers were taken to the place where they committed the robbery, and there, in accordance with the custom of the time, hung in chains.

BEEDING CHRISTMAS DINNER DOLE, 1874

Alison Noble draws attention in Beeding – History of a Village *to an 1874 local newspaper description of the Beeding Christmas celebrations catering for the poor and the schoolchildren and featuring the band and the famous Rising Sun Inn, still the focal point of the village:*

There is no country village in West Sussex that enjoys itself more at Christmas than Beeding. This year all the farmers in the parish gave their men a liberal supply of beef, which was no doubt thankfully received. The worthy rector, Dr Bloxam, also gave beef, flour and tea to all the poor in the parish. After that the schoolchildren, numbering nearly 100, were entertained to a grand treat in the way of a Christmas tree, profusely hung with toys and sweets of every description, and also a bountiful supply of oranges and money prizes, which seemed to be heartily enjoyed by all. The band perambulated the town and were entertained at the Rising Sun Inn.

Dr Bloxam sent in the following correction to the newspaper:

I am reported to have given away 'beef, flour and tea' to all the poor ... I am anxious not to gain credit where I do not deserve it. Our annual Christmas dinner dole is the result of a liberal subscription given by the squire of the parish, Mr Bridger, Mr Elliott and Revd Mr Reeves and many others ... The tea was the gift of Mr Scott.

The Rising Sun Inn, Lower Beeding. (Photograph Geoff Doel)

CHRISTMAS CHURCH MUSIC IN THE PAST

By Revd K.H. Macdermott, vicar of Selsey, 1922

The West Gallery Sussex musicians had a fund of Christmas material, much of it self-penned, such as The Ditchling Carol, *composed as late as 1900 by Peter Parsons, with its unusual tempo variations. As their name suggests, these musicians, and the boy singers they accompanied, were accommodated in specially built wooden galleries at the west end of churches, often adjacent to the tower. A number survive, for example at St Nicholas, Portslade, and St Julian, Kingston Buci. The musicians were often of the skilled rural classes who earned enough to be able to afford to buy instruments. In the nineteenth century this form of music came under assault as part of the misguided Victorian assault on forms of traditional music, and were gradually displaced by inferior alternatives. In Sussex the quires lingered longer than in many other counties.*

The Revd K.H. Macdermott, vicar of Selsey, was the foremost authority on Sussex church music and the following extracts are taken from his articles and manuscript papers in the Sussex Archaeological Society Library:

As one result of my researches, I have discovered that no less than twenty different kinds of instruments have been used in Sussex Churches during the past hundred years, viz violin, cello, bass-viol, double-bass, flute, clarionet, oboe, bassoon, serpent, cornet, trumpet, trombone, vamp-horn, barrel organ, chamber organ, harmonium, American organ, pitch-pipe, drum and triangle.

...The flute nearly always figured in the orchestras of Sussex Churches and was often used, when no pitch pipe was available, to sound the note for the choir when singing was unaccompanied. Most of the old flutes were of boxwood, about 2ft in length, with only one key, though sometimes the piccolo (as at Selsey) or short flute was used. At East Lavant there are two flutes in existence, one dated 1821; the other is stated to have been played by a Thomas Wackford in 1824.

The oboe, a double-reed instrument with a penetrating sound, also of boxwood, was not very frequently employed, no doubt on account of the difficulty in playing it. A Sidlesham specimen is of boxwood with ivory rings, and has only two keys.

The somewhat kindred single-reed clarionet was much more common, and most of those that were used had several keys and were thus capable of producing many more notes than the flutes and oboes. One of them formerly played at Sidlesham has no less than twelve keys, an unusual number for an instrument about a century old as this is. A Harting clarionet has only six keys and that of Bosham has no more than one.

Sussex people love nick-names ... The bassoon is a thick wooden double pipe about 4ft in length, always nicknamed the 'horse's leg' in Sussex.

...An instrument that is now practically obsolete in England but still to be met with in France, the Serpent, formed part of Selsey, Heathfield and Upper Beeding bands and probably also of others ... The instrument is of thin wood covered with leather, with a brass trumpet-loke mouthpiece ... With four keys and the usual finger-holes.

...Among books of psalms and hymns formerly used in Sussex were:- *Psalms and Hymn-tunes* by Reinagle (1839) at Hellingly; *The Union Tune Book* at Berwick; Horne's *Psalms and Hymns* at Angmering and Hellingly; Rippon's *Tunes* (1806) at Wilmington; and Dr Addington's *Collection of Psalm Tunes* (1786) at Waldron.

...About 1830 Jevington resolved to have a barrel organ, and a farmer who was a churchwarden was deputed to fetch it in his wagon from London. Also at the same time he was commissioned by his spouse to bring back a new washing machine. Both were duly brought down on a Saturday – but the organ was deposited in the farmhouse kitchen and the washer in the church!

Families

At Waldron the Collins and Unsteads carried on the work for a very long period; at Bosham the Arnold family supplied members of the choir without a break for nearly 90 years, while at Donnington the band at one time was formed of twelve brothers named Davis.

A famous character in and around Henfield in the fifties of last century was one Penniket, whose performances on both clarinet and trombone were noted. He would awake the sleepers in the church by playing the anthem 'Awake, thou that sleepest.'

Pitch

The old pitch must have been much lower than 'Concert' pitch or even 'Normal', for many of the old Anthems and Psalm-tunes are written with a much higher register than modern church music has. I had an old tuning-fork (about 100 years old) which was a semitone lower than concert-pitch.

Sketch of John Pennikott in Woodmancote church, c. 1850. (From *Sussex Church Music in the Past* by K.H. MacDermot)

SOFT SNOW

By William Blake

Termed a 'poet of genius' by T.S. Eliot in his Selected Essays, *1960, the originality and brilliance of the London poet, painter, visionary and engraver William Blake (1757-1827) was generally unrecognised in his own day. One Sussex man, however, William Hayley, a patron of poets and gentleman of means, offered Blake the use of a cottage at Felpham in Sussex. Here Blake, who was often in straitened circumstances, lived for three years rent free with his wife while working on his masterpiece* Milton, A Poem in Two Books. *'Soft Snow' is from* Poems from MSS, *c. 1793:*

I walked abroad in a snowy day:
I ask'd the soft snow with me to play:
She play'd and she melted in all her prime,
And the winter call'd it a dreadful crime.

Sweeping the snow from the doorway, c. 1871.

THE TREES ARE ALL BARE

Sung by Michael Blann,
from Shepherd of the Downs *by Colin Andrews*

Michael Blann was born in 1843 at Upper Beeding and began his shepherding vocation on the South Downs at the age of nine. He was famous as a shepherd and as a traditional singer and acquired much of his extensive repertoire from the famous Sussex sheep fairs such as Findon. He died in 1934 and is buried at Patching. Michael's handwritten songbook, now in the Worthing Museum, includes 'The Trees Are All Bare', a favourite Sussex Christmas song; a variant was collected by Ken Stubbs from George Townshend of Lewes and it is also in the Copper family repertoire. Colin Andrews, himself a fine singer on the Sussex scene in the 1970s, has published an attractive collection of Michael's songs, including this one, with an interesting biographical sketch:

The trees are all bare not one leaf to be seen,
And those meadows their beauty have lost.
As for the leaves, they're all falling from the trees,
And the brooks are all fast-bound by the frost.

The oxen in the yard they are all foddered with straw,
And they send forth their breath like a steam.
The sweetlooking milk maid she finds she must go,
Flakes of ice she finds, she finds all on her cream.

The poor little pigeons sit shivering on the barn,
So cold as the north winds do blow.
The poor innocent sheep from the downs to their fold,
With their fleeces all quite covered with snow.

The poor little small birds to the barn fly for fold,
So silent they rest on the spray.
The poor harmless hare shears the woods for her food,
Leaves her footsteps to show by night and day.

Now Christmas is come and our song we have sung,
Soon comes the spring time of the year.
Come hand around the glass and so let the health go round,
And I wish you all a happy New Year.

A Victorian Christmas card.

BIBLIOGRAPHY

Allen, Andrew: *A Dictionary of Sussex Folk Medicine* (Newbury: Countryside Books, 1995)

Andrews, Colin: *Shepherd of the Downs* (Worthing: Worthing Museum and Art Gallery, 1979)

Beckett, Arthur: *The Wonderful Weald* (London: Mills & Boon, 1911)

Bede: *Ecclesiastical History of the English People* (Harmondsworth: Penguin, 1990)

Beerbohm, Max: *A Christmas Garland* (first edition of this book was printed in 1912)

Bishop, John George: *Brighton Chain Pier* (Brighton: *Brighton Herald*, 1897)

Blencowe, Robert W. (ed.): *The Journal of the Rev. Giles Moore, Rector of Horstead Keynes from the year 1655-1679*

Broadwood, John: *Old English Songs from the Weald of Surrey and Sussex* (London: Balls, 1843)

Brooke, Sam: *Sam Brooke's Journal (1860-1865) – The Diary of a Lancing Schoolboy* (published 1953 by the Friends of Lancing Chapel)

Bushaway, Bob: *By Rite: Custom, Ceremony and Community in England 1700-1880* (London: Junction Books, 1982)

Connell, J.M.: *Lewes, its Religious History* (Lewes London: Baxter Ltd, 1931)

Copper, Bob: *A Song for Every Season* (London: Heinemann, 1971)

Doel, Fran and Geoff: *Mumming, Howling and Hoodening: Midwinter Rituals in Sussex, Kent and Surrey* (Rainham: Meresborough, 1992)

Edius: *Life of St Wilfrid* (Harmondsworth: Penguin, 1981)

Ellman, Edward Boys: *Recollections of a Sussex Parson* (Hove: Combridges, 1912)

Erredge, Herbert: *History and Legend of Bramber Castle* (Bramber: Potter's Museum, undated)

Gibbons, Stella: *Christmas at Cold Comfort Farm and other Stories*

James, Henry: *The Turn of the Screw*, in *The Novels & Tales of Henry James* (New York: Charles Scribner's Sons, 1907-8)

Johnson, W.H.: *Sussex Disasters* (Seaford, S.B. Publications, 1998)

Kaye-Smith, Sheila: *Saints in Sussex* (London, Cassell & Co., 1926)

Kipling, Rudyard: *Rewards and Fairies* (London: Macmillan, 1910)

Latham, Charlotte: *'Some West Sussex Superstitions Lingering in 1868'*, Folk-Lore Record 1 (1878), 1-67

Mede-Fetherstonhaugh, Margaret and OliverWarne: *Up Park and its People* (London: George Allen & Unwin, 1964)

Ogley, Bob, Ian Currie and Mark Davison: *The Sussex Weather Book* (Westerham: Froglets)

Parish, William: (aug Helena Hall): *A Dictionary of the Sussex Dialect* (Bexhill: Gardners, 1981)

Payne, Shaun: *A Sussex Christmas* (Stroud: Alan Sutton, 1990)

Rees, Arthur J.: *Old Sussex and her Diarists* (London: Bodley Head Ltd, 1929)

Salmon, Ann: *Voices of the Village – A History of West Chiltington during the 20th Century* (West Chiltington: West Chiltington Parish Council, 1999)

Simpson, Jacqueline: *Folklore of Sussex* (Stroud: Tempus, 2002)

Stubbs, Ken: *The Life of a Man* (London: EFDSS)

Thirkell, John: *Top Pubs in the South* (London: Imprint, 1976)

Turner, Thomas: *Diary of a Georgian Shopkeeper*

Wales, Tony: *Sussex Ghosts and Legends* (Newbury: Countryside Books, 1992)

Wells, H.G.: *Experiment in Autobiography* (London: Victor Gollancz, 1934)

Women's Insitute Book: *West Wittering* (Chichester: Moore & Wingham, 1930)

Woodford, Cecile: *Portrait of Sussex* (Robert Hale)

INDEX OF EXTRACTS